A BOOK FOR THESE ECONOMIC TIMES

HOW I TURNED
$15,000
INTO
$10,000,000
AND YOU CAN TOO

BUSINESS LESSONS THAT CAN ENRICH YOUR LIFE

RON CUTLER

EZ Editions
Los Angeles

This book is dedicated to:

My Family

And all of you, who have touched my life

INTRODUCTION

This is not your typical business book; it's a mix of a memoir, self-improvement, business ideas and real life stories. It features lessons, principles and ideas that will impact your life and help you on your road to success. You'll be a fly on the wall as I take you through five businesses— all turnarounds or start-ups and all entertainment, leisure or media companies. This means you won't be bored with a giant corporation story or a widget manufacturer or someone who had a rich father to help them get started.

I wrote this book to be entertaining and fun (you may get a few laughs). The book is chock full of information that should significantly increase your chances of business success.

I'm from a lower middle class family, started with zero and built it into millions. I learned business the hard way by making lots of mistakes and learning from them. I didn't have a teacher or mentor to help me, I learned my lessons the best way, through experience and now that experience can be yours. You'll also learn life lessons that could improve your life. The creative process—how to really think outside the box. I'll show you how to manage people contrasting my management style with the greatest businessman of this century—Steve Jobs.

This book is for you if you are:

- Looking to start a business and don't know how to go about it.

- You own a business that has a lot of problems and you're looking at new ways to solve them.
- You're a college student and concerned about getting a job in this tough economic climate. You've read your college text books and now you're ready to experience what the real business world is like. I hope this book gives you ideas that will help you. If you're ready to take the next step, join me as we jump into real life business situations. We'll come up with solutions to problems, overcome fears and increase your chances for success as you learn from my experiences and secrets.
- You're one of the millions of people who've been affected by our economy and want to explore new ways to solve your financial problems. I hope by reading this book it will help kick start your brain into new ways you can solve your financial problems.
- You love listening to radio, worked in radio or are working in radio. This is one book you'll want to read. You'll go behind the scenes, get a real inside look about radio and learn how a radio station is run, how to create radio programs, how to be more creative, how to manage and get the best out of people.

I've created 12 national hit radio shows and services heard by millions of people. I've owned radio stations, radio networks and syndication companies. Now for the first time I will share that experience with you and give you a chance to get inside my head, see how I think, how I create, and handle difficult and challenging situations.

The main reason I wrote this book is to help people attain their goals and dreams. I hope it helps you to do just that.

CHAPTER 1

The Beginning

How it all started

It's hard for me to open-up and share my deepest feelings and thoughts, but my goal is to give to you as many ideas as I can to help you succeed in business and in life. This book is loaded with stories I hope you can enjoy and learn from. I tried not to give you a boring business book, or a text book. My goal is to entertain you, give you an exciting memoir full of ideas and solutions, and give you a laugh or two while providing you with information that I hope impacts your life.

I'm an average guy in every way, and when I do excel, it's because I give my everything to what I'm trying to accomplish.

We all learn our first life lessons from our parents. My dad was a foreman in a printing company and my ma was a house-wife. As a small child, I experienced the continuation of World War II, watching my parents fight it out. My sister Ilene and I would hide in the closet during the times the war raged. It had a big effect on me. I never liked to fight and always looked for conflict resolution, but when that failed, I was prepared in the words of the Godfather, "take it to the mattresses." The lessons of my childhood toughened me up for what was to come.

My mother taught by example: what not to do. I learned to

handle money, never break my promises, and be totally honest in my dealings with other people.

My dad was honest, never lied to me, and told me what was to become my mantra, "What you put into something is what you'll get out of it." I never forgot it, and it was responsible for many future successes.

My dad put limits on himself. Once he thought about buying a small printing company, but changed his mind. Instead, he worked for Brooks Printing for 30 years. When he got cancer and was out of work for six months, he lost his foreman's job. It was then that I started to think about not working for someone else, and most of my life I haven't.

My dad gave me the gift of hard work, and because he never achieved his full potential, I swore I would push myself to the limits of my capacity—and beyond.

In January of 1961, Philadelphia endured the darkest and coldest month of the year. Outside it was freezing; my face felt like the surface of an ice skating rink. Worse, inside our house we had no hot water or heat. My parents had split up and my mother didn't have the money to pay bills. I attempted to attend Temple University while earning enough money to cover our basic necessities. I searched for a job, which was difficult to find. I was desperate and needed money quickly.

They say that, when asked why he robbed banks, Willie Sutton said, "Because that's where the money was." Jesse had it easy. I took a job as a collector for a finance company. I was 18 and assigned the collection territory of North Philadelphia, known for crime, prostitution and drugs. That was my beat: Deadbeat. My job's mission was to collect money from people who were way behind in their payments.

Principle: It's not how much you bill out, it's how much you collect.

The company didn't allow you to use your own surname, so I looked for the nearest street sign—Diamond Street. I became Ron Diamond. At America Finance, the company measured your job performance on IR's—immediate results. If you collected a payment, you were credited with an IR. I had a 97% IR rating, the highest in the office and I was told the highest in the country. So how did a naïve inexperienced kid succeed?

> **Principle: If you don't know you can't succeed, you very well might.**

I was determined, honest and empathetic. I devised a strategy: I cared about the plight of the people I was assigned to collect from. I couldn't afford to see these folks as "reluctant customers." It wasn't "them versus us." The healthier perspective in sales is to realize "It's all us." So I approached each of them, not as a collector, but as someone who was interested in their problems. Why were they having trouble paying their bills? How much of a payment could they afford to make? If they couldn't make a payment, when could they pay? (When they paid, it turned into an IR). I was riveted listening to them tell me about their problems.

> **Principle: Listen and care about others. Your success depends on it.**

I genuinely cared. After all, I was poor too. My clients perceived me as someone who listened to them and suggested ways to handle their financial problems. Perception's important. And when it matches reality it's called integrity. My approach may have been "unorthodox" but my results were right on the money, literally. Of course, nothing is perfect. I had a client who promised a small payment when I returned the following week. The day arrived and Ms. Jones was in an ornery mood. She pulled out a nine-inch kitchen knife, chased me out of her house and followed me down the street.   Luckily, I ran track in high school. She ran fast, I ran faster. She was one of the three percent from whom I never collected money owed. But at least I was breathing, and ready to continue my journey from poverty to riches.

Principle: Always be on your toes, ready to make your move at a moment's notice.

The title of my book: *How I Turned $15,000 Into $10,000,000* only pertains to the $15,000 I used to start *Cutler Productions* and doesn't include the money I made from the other businesses mentioned in this book.   Many of you don't have $15,000, but don't let that stop you. I started my first business venture with $25 given to me by my Aunt Betty. Aunt Betty never had any children; I was like the son she never had. Aunt Betty's nickname was Bingo Betty because she played bingo eight nights a week. Years later I treated Aunt Betty to many Las Vegas trips. The casinos loved her—she always lost. It didn't bother Aunt Betty; she enjoyed the thrill of gambling and never lost more than she could afford. Loving and generous, she was always special to me. I used the $25 she gave me to start my first teenage dance. It was a one-night success and I used the profits from that dance to start another dance. It seemed every time I had a successful dance, problems and obstacles beyond my control closed the dances. These obstacles never stopped me— and you shouldn't let them stop you. After two years of one dance after another, I finally struck gold. In the next chapter you'll follow my teenage dances (called record hops at the time) and see me get knocked down many times, get up again, and eventually overcome many obstacles on my road to riches.

I chose to start my first business venture—teenage dances, because I was a dancer, had a passion for music, and loved the idea of being a disc jockey. When the door of opportunity opened, I took advantage of it.

> **Principle: When the door of Opportunity opens for you, make sure you go through it.**

I hadn't started my first business yet, but I was already learning some important lessons.

On the Road to Success:

1. *You must have a burning desire to succeed. It's essential to overcoming obstacles. How do you get a burning desire? Do what you love.*

2. *Motivation is one of the major keys to success. Find your motivation and use it to take action. What's your motivation?*

3. *Make sure you have a passion for your business choice and love doing it. Be certain your choice is based on a skill or talent you possess.*

4. *You must have a plan and strategy. (I'll have more information and ideas about this in later chapters.)*

5. *No matter what business you choose to enter or start, remember that success starts with good communication between people. Work on your communication skills and remember—your goal should be to enrich the lives of the people you encounter.*

6. *Genuinely care about your customers and employees. Make sure you put them first; your road to success will be easier.*

CHAPTER 2

Developing a Personal Brand

In this Chapter:

- How to develop your own personal brand
- Persevere
- Watch me fail
- Not let failure stop you
- Overcome Obstacles

June 1962

Hy Lit, the top AM radio DJ in Philadelphia at the time, had left the Playland Roller Skating Rink in the Port Richmond section of Philly to run a dance at suburban Willow Grove Amusement Park.

Vince, the owner of Playland, didn't know what to do. His dance attendance had fallen from 1000 teenagers down to 232. It was summertime and teens had headed for the beach in Wildwood, New Jersey or street corners to hang out. Vince knew about me from his friend Peter, who also owned a skating rink. Peter knew I was a go-getter—I made extra bucks booking skating parties for him and he knew I loved dances. I had no experiences as a dance DJ. I never did it before, but I was eager to try. I danced at many record hops, knew the type of kids who attended them and the songs teens loved to dance to. I was lucky; Vince had no other alternative but to give me a chance. He hired me for one week and if I didn't work out, I'd be out the door. You don't look a gift horse in the mouth, even if it seems lame at the time. I remembered the name I used when I worked at American Finance—Ron Diamond. I created the moniker "the rock in rock'n roll is a diamond" and jumped at the opportunity.

When Saturday arrived, the usual 200 teens showed up along with the chance to prove myself. As soon as I took the stage and looked out over the crowd below, I transcended from a 19 year-old nobody into a celebrity in the eyes of the kids. I danced on stage and pleased the crowd by playing song requests and taking dedications. They responded by spreading the word, creating a buzz that the new disc jockey at Playland was cool. Attendance began creeping up.

After the first night of the Playland dance, I felt different about myself. I grew up being just one of the crowd. But that night was momentous. I underwent a transformation that led to a better self-image. On the stage at Playland, I became special, a feeling I had rarely experienced before. I never had a desire to be a disc jockey, but in a flash I became one.

Life is full of unexpected surprises and events; they happened to me and I'm sure they've happened to you.

Now, I was determined to build the crowd. I decided on a strategy and the tactics that would execute that strategy. I was like a politician running a campaign, going from one teen hangout to another and encouraging kids to dance at Playland. But this time I wasn't collecting debts, I was collecting customers. I gave out flyers and hung posters on telephone poles. It was grassroots, personal street-level marketing. Today it's called guerilla marketing. I had started at Playland the last Saturday in June and by the end of August the crowd had risen to over 1200. Still, I took home just $25 dollars a night. Should I have demanded more? In today's world of short-term goals with short-term gains, it might seem like the right thing. Instead, I demanded more of myself.

> **Principle: Short-term goals and gains may seem important, but achieving longer-term goals is the true road to riches.**

I had the teens fill out index cards with their names, addresses and phone numbers. I collected 2,000 names and used them to build my first data bank—in a shoebox. I began to build my personal brand: Ron Diamond. I gave the teens what they wanted: played great dance music [product], communicated with them, and cared about their dedications and requests [customer service]. This led to them having a great time. It also began the building of the Ron Diamond Dances, which, in the coming years, over one million would attend, and which would take me from poverty to riches.

> **Principle: Add value to your personal brand and don't wait for someone else to promote or reward you. You're the boss.**

Spring 1963

LITHUANIAN HALL—LOCATION, LOCATION, LOCATION [From life to death in one night]

I left Playland and started my own dance that had the potential to make me a decent amount of money. I was young and never feared failure. I had built confidence from my experience promoting the Playland dance, and based on that, I felt I could succeed. My Aunt Betty contributed $25 [she previously had given me $25 for Playland posters and flyers that kicked started my business career]. I spent $150 of my own money, and initiated a Friday night dance at the Lithuanian Music Hall, in an location close to my Playland following. I wasn't yet on the radio, which put me at a huge competitive disadvantage against other DJ's. So I used the 1963 version of "My Space": I sent out 2000 penny post cards to my mailing list and handed out flyers at neighborhood high schools. Friday night arrived and, to my surprise, 1400 teens showed up at a Ron Diamond Dance.

I was on my way, I thought. I netted over $1100 dollars for one night's work. Had I asked my old boss at Playland to double my salary to $50, rather than taking the risk and putting sweat equity into my new venture, I'd never have realized my greater potential. I was on my way...but for one problem: The Lithuanian Hall was next door to a mortuary, which was holding a wake the night of my dance.

Running your own business is said to be a life and death proposition, but I always thought it was more of a metaphor. The owner of the mortuary was understandably upset to see hundreds of teens assembled in front of his funeral home. He let the Lithuanian Hall know how disturbed he was, and my Friday night schedule of dances was cancelled. But I was determined not to let it be a nail in my coffin.

Principle: Embrace your obstacles in order to achieve your goal. Never give up. Obstacles are part of your challenge—you will always have obstacles. How you handle them is up to you.

AMITY HALL [Driving your customers to the store]

October 1963

It's hard getting locations for teen dances. Later in 1963, I found a hall in Pennsauken, New Jersey, across the Tacony Palmyra Bridge and ten miles from Port Richmond. The area was a new market for me. I put flyers on the buses of three high schools in the area. At the time, Pennsauken was considered a suburb of Philly. How do you drive trusted customers to a new location? I took the question *literally*. I rented a bus and took 50 of my dancers from Northeast Philadelphia to Amity Hall. The building was small and only had a capacity of 400. I sandwiched 500 teens into the place and turned away several hundred. I rented the hall for $25 and hired a private detective agency to run security. After all expenses, I made $350 profit. Things went well the next three weeks as capacity crowds danced their hearts out.

On the fifth week I was driving to my Sunday afternoon dance at Amity Hall when I turned on the radio and heard that the NAACP planned to demonstrate at a dance hall in Pennsauken. Not mine, I thought. I had never heard from them nor did I do anything that would give them a reason to picket. When I arrived, I found I was mistaken. I discovered that one of my security guards had told a teenager he couldn't come in because he was a black. I fired the guard immediately.

The first hour of the dance was uneventful. The usual capacity crowd was there. At 3PM, one hour after the hop started, five station wagons pulled up across the street. 20 black teenagers and seven adult protesters got out. I immediately went outside, explained the situation, and invited the teens to come inside as my guests and dance for free. There was some tension inside,

11

but there were no disturbances. I thought I had dodged the bullet. Instead, I wound up biting it.

I was never prejudiced and naively thought most of the world felt the same. When I was growing up, my playmates included five Jews, three Christians and two African-Americans. I grew up playing with my friends nearly every day and never felt any differences between us. We all got along great. So when the race problems at Amity Hall surfaced, I was upset. At the time, I knew if I did the right thing, I would lose the dance. Even though I needed the money, my ethics and morals trumped the dollars I would have made. I decided to make the right choice.

Remember, this was 1963, a year before the Civil Rights Act. I was notified later in the week that Amity Hall was canceling my dances. I'm convinced the cause was my actions that Sunday afternoon in October 1963, one month before the John F. Kennedy assassination. I was discouraged and disheartened but I would not give up. Sooner or later, if I persisted, my luck would change.

Principle: People screw up. You can still act responsibly with integrity. How you react is up to you. Circumstances may be beyond your control, but you always have control over your reaction to them.

OVERCOMING OBSTACLES, ISSUES AND CHALLENGES IN A SMART AND DECENT WAY ARE ESSENTIAL IF YOU WANT TO SUCCEED IN BUSINESS.

WAYS TO OVERCOME OBSTACLES:
Define the obstacle or problem confronting you.

- *What's stopping you? Be clear and precise.*
- *Ask yourself what you really want, regardless of whether you think it's possible. (Be honest and see what comes up for you.)*
- *Let your mind go wild and list as many ideas as you can to get you what you want. Focus on what you want and don't be a victim of the problem.*
- *Look at the list of your solutions and pick the strongest one.*
- *If you're still uncomfortable with the answer, talk to people you trust and get their ideas. (They may have a fresh perspective and come up with a solution you didn't think of.)*

DIAMOND'S DEN [inspiration meets perspiration]

January 1964

The Beatles invaded the USA with their first number one song, *"I Wanna Hold Your Hand."*

I still didn't have anyone holding my hand, so my struggle to succeed continued. I found an industrial warehouse in the far northeast area of Philadelphia. I called the place Diamond's Den and started doing dances there on Sunday afternoons. I had succeeded in drawing good crowds in my previous attempts at establishing a regular dance, but every time I had been stopped by circumstances beyond my control. This one seemed like a sure winner. The warehouse held over 1600 people and there were no neighbors nearby. I did my normal promotion: postcards to my mailing list, flyers to all the target high schools, 100 posters on area telephone poles and visits to the key teen hangouts. My promotion and marketing were by pure instinct; I didn't know at the time that I was learning skills that one day would lead to giant payoffs.

> **Principle: Once you've tried to outthink yourself and consulted the experts, try common sense. You'll discover it's not all that common.**

Sunday afternoon arrived and a capacity crowd showed up. They say "the more the merrier." I say, be careful of what "they" say. The 1600 teenagers dancing up a storm were also causing intense heat and energy, and suddenly the tile floor began to sweat. Minute by minute water began to collect and rise. After two hours the kids were dancing in nearly two inches of water. Maybe I should have changed the dress code to bathing suits only. Great marketing, excellent product, defective packaging. The dance died of drowning—giving a whole new meaning to "sweat equity."

It took courage and persistence for me to carry on. Every time I started a successful dance, circumstances beyond my control intervened and I lost it. Obstacles are part of life, particularly in business. I figured if I continued to work hard my luck would change. At least I was absorbing important lessons that would later contribute to my success. I was frustrated, but I wouldn't let that stop me. I was on a mission to succeed. The failures lit the fire of my determination and it continued to grow into energy that I knew would eventually produce results. Finally, after three years of struggles things were about to change.

STARLITE BALLROOM WILDWOOD
Summer 1964—*(The Big Break)*

Whether it's bum luck or dumb luck, you've seen that there are always wild cards that come up in getting any business off the ground.

> **Principle: It's not what you're dealt; it's how you play your hand.**

I never believed in the phrase "Due to circumstances beyond our control." That was television's excuse flying in the face of the showbiz homily, "The show must go on." To a great extent, for the entrepreneur, all business is show business. Those who believe in fate will tell you "there are no coincidences." Maybe so, but to the contrary, I say, "there are only coincidences." At any given moment in your business journey, certain elements are in play and available to you. How you choose to make the most of those pivotal moments will determine your future and define your character. Keep going. Stay alert. Don't give up.

I had started on the boardwalk, but it was still a long way from Park Place.

I heard that the legendary Starlight Ballroom on the boardwalk in Wildwood, New Jersey, was looking for a disc jockey to replace Dick Clark, who had left Philly for Southern California. I could have thought, I'm no star brand. I haven't any radio exposure, OR, I could have imagined myself filling Clark's dancing shoes.

> **Principle: The choice you make about yourself informs the choice you make about your business growth. Ask "Why not me?" and slay the imagined obstacles before you make them real.**

It was March. Two months later, the town would explode with thousands of people celebrating Memorial Day weekend. Now, though, it was cold, and bleak—a ghost town. I drove down to the Hunt Brothers' offices. They owned all the theaters and most of the amusement attractions at the time in Wildwood,

New Jersey, including the Starlight Ballroom. I was determined to be Dick's replacement. I met with Bud Dry, the manager, and convinced him of my success with my previous dances. Most of the Northeast Philly teenagers spent their summer vacations on the Jersey shore in Wildwood. When Bud checked me out, he found I did have a following, and those packed, failed dances finally paid off. He hired me for $150 a week to work five nights.

Friday night of Memorial Day Weekend was the opening night. I didn't know it at the time, but that weekend was an audition to see if I would get the gig for the summer. Friday night we had a good crowd (1400), Saturday 2000 and Sunday another 1400. The kids gave me a warm response and the Hunt Brothers hired me for the summer. Starlight had a large marquee on the boardwalk that overlooked the tens of thousands that passed by. There, in large letters was TEENAGE DANCE FEATURING RON DIAMOND. The brand (Ron Diamond) was beginning to happen. I stayed in a $15-a-week rooming house over the Emerald Room night club and lived on 15-cent hot dogs so I could save money. By the end of the summer, I had saved over $1200. I was joyous; I finally had money in the bank—but not for long. In September my mother hadn't made mortgage payments in eight months and the bank was about to foreclose. I took the money I had saved and paid what was owed. My mother lived in that house another 31 years.

CONCORD—Ron Diamond to the Rescue
[finally, a home run]

Friday, October 9, 1964

The Concord was a large roller skating rink at 7049 Frankford Avenue in the Mayfair section of Philadelphia. In

1962, Hy Lit ran a successful dance that attracted over 2000 teens every Friday night. Then the nemesis of all teenage activities happened: all hell broke loose—fights, noise that upset neighbors, and teenage drinking. This wasn't the fault of Hy's or the management of Concord's, but as they said, "Lit happens". The neighbors petitioned the city to close the dance. After pressure and falling attendance because of the adverse publicity, the Lescas brothers, the owners of Concord, closed the dance and fought the city's attempt to revoke their dance license. The Lescas won and Concord still had its license, but how would they attempt to woo the dancers back? Enter Ron Diamond. I studied the problem: good location, bad reputation.

Principle: Learn to take the good with the bad. Then teach yourself how to flip the bad into good.

Here's how I did it, with a lot of "what ifs." It's a form of brainstorming—let your mind go free and start writing down everything that comes to you. Don't judge until you've exhausted all your possible solutions. Then start eliminating the ones that are weakest until you get to the one you feel is the strongest. This technique isn't original...millions of people use it, but back in 1964, the technique came to me instinctively. It's a part of critical thinking, which will help you on the road to business success. You have to consider the downsides with the ups, but at the same time, you can't let the downside scenarios bring you down. Remember the optimism and the source of the juice that got you going on this venture in the first place. Once you lose that connection, you're forever lost. Once you reconnect, you become more resilient, more resourceful, and your chances of self-generated success increase exponentially.

17

The Solution:

I suggested we target college-age students and make them wear coats and ties. It was a radical idea at the time, but I knew if kids dressed up they would be less inclined to fight, and be on their best behavior. I also decided to use live bands, with a DJ between music sets. I visited all the colleges in the Metro Philadelphia area: Temple, Penn, LaSalle, Beaver (where the hot girls were) and others. I visited all their student centers, promoting Concord as the place to be. I hired Tina and the Marquis, a popular band at the time. The first night we drew 600, and a month later 1000. We never had fights or any trouble. The neighbors noticed the well-dressed, well-behaved teens and appreciated the change.

Principle: Always monitor your performance. Keep what works, discard what used to work and doesn't anymore. Attach yourself to success, not just tradition. You create and run your own patterns, they don't run you.

After several months, the live bands' popularity waned. I dropped them and went with the market-driven choice. Most of the dancers preferred dancing to a DJ spinning the hottest tunes of the day. The crowd began to change—less college, more local teens. Those who used to dance at Concord began showing up, boys wearing coats and ties and girls in dresses. No one misbehaved. I was now the sole attraction, spinning records and making sure all that attended burned holes in their soles and had a tremendous time. The crowd grew to over 1400, and in 1966, when I had a radio show; it grew to 2200 capacity every Sunday night for four straight years. I owned a piece of the box office and for the first time in my life I had a substantial income. My

Aunt Betty's $25 investment returned $75,000 in benefits to her for the rest of her life, as well as the six-figure income I earned yearly over those years (none of which is counted in the ten million I was to make later in my life.) My "day job" was to work nights and weekends.

Principle: It's not just long hours that make success; it's knowing the right hours to work.

Concord conquered.

On the Road to Success:

You've just read stories where I mostly failed, usually from circumstances beyond my control. But I didn't let it stop me; I kept going till I succeeded. I hope these stories inspire and help you on your road to success.

19

CHAPTER 3

In this Chapter:

- *Learn how I climbed the mountain and learned how to conquer my specific industry.*
- *Find out who your targeted customers are and what they want.*
- *Choose not to follow the crowd (other similar businesses) and dare to be different and unique.*
- *Find your unique selling proposition (USP) (your business' selling advantage) and make sure that it gives you a competitive edge.*
- *Learn to use decision-making to your advantage.*

Radio—Roll over Beethoven— Diamond Hits the Airways WIFI

4th Quarter of 1965

I started out literally pounding the pavement. I visited my clients one-to-one. I put up a hundred posters one at a time. I made what was then a substantial living "in person." But you can only be in one place at one time. The old saying "if you're within the sound of my voice" meant I needed a bigger megaphone. I knew my market (teenagers) and I knew myself. My maverick, grassroots style wasn't one to get me on a corporate major market radio station, yet I knew DJs were folk heroes.

I always loved radio, and listened to the top radio personalities of the day. I remember those hot summer nights sitting on my doorstep and imagining having my own show. I didn't want to be a time and temperature jock. I wanted the freedom to choose the songs I played, including those that deserved airplay, but didn't have the clout or money behind them to get on the traditional Top 40 stations. If I went on the radio, I could promote my dances and attendance would increase dramatically. So I created a unique radio personality who would play songs you didn't hear on other radio stations.

> **Principle: If you're the new guy on the block, against the successful and established guy (company), use a flanker position. Don't do what they're offering unless you can do it a lot better. Flanker position is what you do differently and offers advantages and benefits the big guy (company) isn't offering.**

In 1965, FM radio was home to beautiful music or elevator music, ethnic programming, block programming (all types of different programs) or any program someone was willing to pay for airtime that would allow a radio station owner to survive.

In Philadelphia, WDVR, a beautiful music station, was not only the number one-rated FM station at the time, but claimed they had the largest audience of any FM station in America.

Somebody had to be a pioneer and offer contemporary and oldies music on FM. To my knowledge, at the time no radio station in the nation had programmed it. I knew my task would be difficult. FM penetration in Philadelphia was 17% (meaning only 17% of the market had FM receivers.)

My dancers were constantly asking me when I would be on the radio. WIBG-990AM, Hy Lit's home base, was the only top 40 station in the market. It had tremendous ratings and a loyal audience. I hadn't a chance of getting hired there—and didn't want to—they played only the top pop hits. My instincts were to play songs that hit home with the kids, even if they didn't hit the top of the charts: dance tunes, soul hits, some Top 40 and oldies.

> **Principle: If you do what you love, sometimes you've got to go it alone.**

Sometimes when you follow your heart, it'll lead you right to the bank. Besides, I needed a unique facet to my personal brand. I called them "Diamond exclusives" (songs I loved but weren't heard on radio stations).

> **Principle: Being different will make you stand out. Being different and better will let you stand tall. Dare to be better.**

In late 1965, I found a 50,000 watt FM station in Philadelphia called WIFI. It featured ethnic programming, Broadway music and every type of paid-for program imaginable. I went to visit Mel Gollub, the owner, in Norristown, Pennsylvania and convinced him to let me have a show on Saturday and Sunday nights. I sold advertising to four sponsors guaranteeing Mel much-needed revenue. I finally had a radio program that gave me a platform to promote my dances and to compete with the big name disc jockeys in the market. But being on the radio is no guarantee you'll have anyone tune in. The program leading into mine was a polka show, hosted by Polka Joe, and as much as my audience loved dance music, polka wasn't cool.

In early 1966, Arbitron, the radio ratings company, listed stations with little or no audience, and gave them a rating of minus one (the joke in the business was that it meant no one was listening to you, and the person on the air was busy listening to another station when his mike wasn't on). WIFI, like so many other FM radio stations at the time, had that dubious honor.

Across the FM dial in America I couldn't find another station that had a programming idea similar to mine. I had low expectations considering the number of FM sets in the market; young people never listened to FM. But I had what they call today a "killer ap." That's when a new medium (like Xbox) doesn't take off until there's a piece of content (like "Halo") that encourages people to buy the hardware.

> **Principle: Give people something they really want and they'll break the inertia between desire and fulfillment.**

My following of Ron Diamond dancers, numbering in the thousands, found ways to purchase FM radios allowing them to tune in and get the unique content they craved. They felt special and they spread the word (today they would call it viral). I promoted the radio show at the dances, and on the radio I promoted the hops. It was a perfect marriage of marketing: product, people and promotion.

> **Principle: Provide the honey and the buzz will start and take on a life of its own.**

I was not homogenized and not sanitized like my competition. (Much later, Howard Stern took it to an extreme). I was wild, crazy and uninhibited, and I only played about 30% of the songs played on WIBG 98 (the better songs). I eliminated records that I thought didn't match the image I was portraying (even songs I might have liked). I knew I wasn't playing on a level playing field, so I chose to create a similar but unique game on a funkier, but adjacent playing field.

The strategy I used was a classic flanker position. It's been used in many types of businesses to help them succeed. I countered WIBG by positioning myself as the wildest personality in the market. I created characters like my talking turntables—Romeo and Juliet. To add a little drama and conflict I created an organization determined to remove me from the radio dial: B.L.U.N.D.E.R. standing for Beethoven Lovers United Nationally to Destroy Ever-lasting Rock 'n Roll. I took dedications and requests and I did a "make or break portion" where the audience voted if I should play the record or not. If they didn't like the song, I would break it over my microphone. I talked to my listeners, not at them. Whenever I had the opportunity, I reached out to touch the audience's emotions with introductions to songs. I had Frenchy the kissing horn, a weird sound that signaled guys to kiss the girls they were with. It's amazing how many guys would park their car and turn on 92.5. I had 38,000 card carrying V.I.L.'s (Very Important Listeners). Dancers signed up to get they're cards at the dances. I called myself the Diamond, "the rock in rock n' roll". I used the monikers "the cool jewel, the stone with tone and the atomic mouth." Many of the things I did may sound corny today, but they worked at the time.

Every night I made sure to play a song dedicated to our fighting men in Vietnam; there were hundreds who had been Ron Diamond listeners. Yes the war was unpopular, but I believed we owed it to our guys over there to support them. Soldier Boy by Shirley and the Shirelles was always the night's most requested song.

**Principle: Don't be afraid to be corny.
Hip businesses fold just as fast as others do.**

After two weeks, Mel put me on the radio seven nights a week. In addition to the Concord dance, I began doing high school dances all over the Delaware Valley attended by thousands, thanks to my WIFI radio show. As long as the show was a vehicle to bring in customers to my dances and it worked, ratings didn't matter. I lived and died by the revenue, not the ratings. Traditionally, the product of most radio stations is not the format or the content of the shows. The product of most radio stations is the listeners. That's because the number of listeners are sold to advertisers and that's the station's source of revenue. Because my goal was different, and I knew it, my content was different. Sometimes, though, in reaching one goal, you will achieve unexpected bonuses.

The radio show skyrocketed attendance at the dances. The hops were wall-to-wall with dancers dancing their asses-off. If the big-name jocks on the top-rated am stations WIBG or WFIL made the mistake of competing directly with me, they soon regretted it. My dances remained at capacity with or without competition. (it was all about branding—when it came to dances, Ron Diamond Dances' brand was like Coke).

In 1966 there were sixteen AM radio stations and almost as many FM stations in the Philadelphia metro market. Many had big promotional budgets for buses, billboards and TV. One day during my show, Mel came into the studio with a giant smile pasted on his face.

"Why are you so happy?" I said.

"For the first time in our station's history we have ratings in Arbitron."

"Congratulations." I sat uncomfortably in my chair, hoping I helped get those ratings. "So no more minus ones."

Mel shuffled his feet and was silent for a moment.

"We still had minus ones in all day parts except seven to midnight, when you were on." Mel hesitated for a second, adding a little dramatic tension to the situation.

"You tied WDVR as the number one FM in the market and

beat fifteen of the sixteen AM's. It's amazing. You have no lead-in or lead out show. We don't have a consistent format and you still got those ratings. WIBG was the only station with higher numbers."

That didn't surprise me—they had great jocks and they played the same music 24 hours a day. They also were a Top 40 station for nine years and had garnered an enormous audience. My ratings came during the first six months I was on the air and were a harbinger that FM radio had arrived. In less than a year there would be FM Top 40 or Rock stations in most markets in America.

In the spring of 1967, Herb Scott, owner of several radio stations, asked if I would like to work at his station in Trenton, WTTM-AM. The station's signal blanketed Northeast Philadelphia and four northern and eastern counties, a stronghold of my listeners and dancers. In the rest of the Philly metro the signal was either weak, poor or nonexistent. Legendary comedian Ernie Kovacs had worked at the station in the 50's, and some of the country's best Top 40 jocks had started there. Mr. Scott gave me free rein to do, say and play what I wanted.

A new Top 40 radio station, WFIL, had entered the Philadelphia market in late 1966 and immediately battled WIBG. I liked the challenge of the Trenton market because I would compete not only with the two Philly stations, but also against the legendary Cousin Brucie at WABC and B. Mitchell Reed at WMCA, New York. These stations could also be heard in the Trenton metro. There was one Top 40 station in Trenton, WAAT, a daytime station. WTTM had a "middle of the road" music format during the day, and, if I took the job, I would be rockin' at night. My dilemma was, do I stay at WIFI or go to WTTM?

My income from the stations wasn't important. I promoted my dances on my show and that was where the money was:

27

packing the dances (at the time, I was making as much money as the leading pros on the PGA tour, of course, they were making a small fraction of the leading golfers of today).

Decision making:

The scenario: WTTM or stay at WIFI

It was decision time. Many of my dancers still didn't have FM radios. The Concord, my Sunday night dance, was packing them in and WTTM covered my market area well. 95 percent of my income came from the dances. AM Top 40 stations in 1967 still dominated the ratings. If I joined WTTM, I would open new dance markets in Bucks, Mercer, Burlington and Camden Counties. In Trenton, I had a chance to battle the other radio stations and be number one while making a strong statement. WIFI had stopped growing because of the emergence of WFIL. A chance to take on four of the biggest Top 40 jocks in the country tempted me. After weighing all the factors, I decided to take my chances and leave for WTTM.

Decision-making is a real challenge—it's one of the most important ingredients to success in life and in business.

> **Principle: When you have a decision, don't make it quickly. Instead, focus on all the details required to make the right choice. List the positives and negatives. Which factors will help you achieve your goals and get you what you want? (We'll have more on decision making at the end of this chapter.)**

My WTTM radio show burst into the market, thanks to my former audience from WIFI and the dancers from my hops, which mushroomed into a huge audience in less than a month.

I was on the air from 9PM to 11:30 Monday-Friday. When I couldn't do the shows live (because of the dances) I taped them. I began executing my strategy. I added a Saturday night dance at Edgely Fire Hall in Levittown, Pennsylvania, another dance at the War Memorial in Trenton and Friday nights at different high schools in my coverage area. I now had hops every Friday, Saturday and Sunday night. When the summer came, I did dances seven nights a week, adding an extra night to Edgely's and additional locations the other nights. On nights when I had two dances, I would make sure I appeared at one of them early for at least an hour and then handed off to one of my trained assistants. I would then drive to the next dance and D.J the final ninety minutes. I was lucky—I never was sick or missed a dance in seven years. I had a great deal of energy; it helped that I was in my early twenties.

On Mondays, I walked into the bank with dollar bills in large shopping bags. You knew I was coming because one-by-one the tellers rushed to grab the "closed" sign and put them on their windows. That's how I made my living, a dollar at a time. In the summer, during a good week, over 10000 teenagers danced at my dances.

How did I do it?

Using my popular radio show to promote my dances helped. On occasion, my hops went head to head with dances headlining a DJ from WFIL or WIBG. They were able to get recording stars to appear at their record hops, which I wasn't. It didn't matter. My dances drew over 1000, while my competition was lucky to draw 100. So it was more than the radio promotion. The secret was branding Ron Diamond. Guys knew there would be wall-to-wall girls at a Ron Diamond dance. The girls were attracted because I played the right selection of music, blended together in the right order to set the right mood. The dances featured the kids, not me. Many danced on the stage. I would do countless dedications and requests and always had as my goal to give the teens attending a good time—more than their money's worth.

> **Principle: Dollars don't spend themselves, people do. Customers shell out only when they think they're getting their money's worth.**

My job at WTTM made me more socially aware. I felt I had a responsibility to the community. It was more than entertaining and playing great songs on the radio or at great record hops—it was the good deeds I could do.

In 1968, I stayed on the air for 24 consecutive hours to raise money for Multiple Sclerosis. This was the first Multiple Sclerosis radiothon and was soon duplicated by radio stations across the country. The governor of New Jersey awarded me a plaque.

> **Principle: What's good for the ego may or may not be good for business, but what's good for the soul will strengthen you when you need it most. It's the part of business where you do good deeds for your community and nourish your soul, not your pocketbook.**

I read an article in the now-defunct Philadelphia Bulletin newspaper about kids no one wanted to adopt because they had physical or mental handicaps. It was Christmas time. I read the article on the air and in two hours over $5000 was raised from my audience. I distributed the money to three orphanages, which used the dollars to buy Christmas gifts for the children. I had a little money left over and heard about a woman whose husband had left her with their twelve children. She didn't have any money or food for Christmas. I added some of my own to what I had left and showed up on Christmas Eve with food and gifts for all her children, plus extra money for the woman. I will never forget the smiles on the woman and children's faces. It was the favorite Christmas of my life.

WTTM'S general manager, Ed Ramsey, told me when he listened to the show he always held his breath and prayed I wouldn't do or say something that would bring the FCC to his door. I never did.

I still was wild and crazy on the air, coming close but never crossing the line. I used a lot of double-entendre's (words that had double meetings). I knew the teenage mind and knew how they would interpret it. My goal was to entertain them and give them an occasional laugh. I also played novelty songs like "My Ding-a-ling" and other songs that may have been risqué at the time, but would be G rated in today's world. Every show ended with Parkology: 30 minutes of love songs. Many teens wrote me that they had their first real kiss when Parkology was on. I'm basically a quiet guy. But when I got in front of a microphone, I became uninhibited.

But the real secret of Ron Diamond was the music I played. If you talk to my listeners, I'm sure the thing they would remember the most was the music: the song selections and the way the songs were put together.

In 1969, the Trenton riots broke out and made front page headlines in newspapers coast to coast. I had large audiences in both the Black and Italian communities. I quietly worked behind the scenes to cool down the situation. I called for calm and dialogue and used the platform of my radio show as a voice of reason.

Principle: If you have the opportunity, be sure to do public service.

Hooper, a radio rating service (no longer in business), released the Trenton market ratings. I had a 49% share of the market. The two Philly Top 40 stations and the two New York Top 40 stations combined had lower numbers. I owned the market.

> **Principle: When the big guys are fighting to reach the mainstream, find an opening for your niche. You can own the market without being the biggest player, just the smartest one.**

The dances were packing them in and the radio ratings were at all-time highs, but I was tired and bored. For the previous five years I had taken only one vacation. I worked seven nights a week and knew I didn't want to be a radio and dance personality the rest of my life. I loved what I was doing, but something deep inside of me told me it was time to make a change. I was ready for a lifestyle change and wanted to reinvent myself.

> **Principle: Change is part of life. Don't be afraid of it. If you feel in your heart and soul you need it, do it.**

In April of 1970, I decided to vacation in California. I drove from San Francisco to San Diego. Along the way, I fell in love with California. I called my former boss Mel at WIFI and asked if he was interested in partnering with me to buy a California FM station. He said yes. The choice came down to two stations—one in San Diego and the classical music station in San Jose, KRPM. I left San Diego and flew back to San Jose.

Do you know the way to San Jose? I wish I hadn't.

1971 was one of the toughest years of my life. From air personality to the desk of General Manager, my income was reduced by 80% from what I made from the dances. I chose a format (Album-oriented Rock) I wasn't prepared for and I entered a world different than the world in which I grew up. I'm not sure I would do it again, but on the positive side, struggle and negative experiences can be a positive experience if you learn from them—and I did.

It was decision time:

The San Jose FM was priced right...$240,000, and its market's population growth was impressive. The market was exciting, and as part of the greater San Francisco metro market, had additional appeal. San Diego also had spectacular population growth and a better climate. I consulted media brokers and other experts and they recommended the San Jose market. I chose San Jose, but in hindsight, I should have chosen San Diego. I was unaware of the surprising challenges and crises I would soon face.

On the Road to Success:

Below is a principle that helped me position my business and develop a unique advantage. I've used it every time I start a business or battle a competitor—it worked for me and I hope it will work for you.

> **Principle: Market share is where you stand in the pack. If you have no market share, use positioning: Stand next to the market leader and play up your differences as benefits. It's much easier for the customer to shift the status quo than the market leader to change. Be flexible and bend in the direction the wind's blowing.**

Here's another idea I gained from my experiences.

Although it's always a good idea to be prepared and seek expert advice before starting a new business, remember this: An expert may be defined as one who is up-to-date with the latest information and has studied deeply on the subject. However, just because one is well-informed, there's no guarantee that he will come up with the wisest conclusion. Even experts disagree. Gather knowledge like an expert but think like a businessman. Experts' opinions may carry weight, but you're the one who has to carry the water.

Earlier in the chapter, I told you I would give you more information about decision –making. Below are more questions to ask and more ideas to help you on the road to business success.

Decision-Making

Risk assessment is important in decision-making. Make sure you compare your risk to reward. Look at the problem from all sides: business, personal, health, psychological, and make sure you weigh your chances for success. (When I'm making a decision, I always take time to write down the pros and cons. It leads to better decision-making).

Ask yourselves these questions:

What's your competition?

Is there a market for your product or services and who are your targeted consumers?

What are the demographics (age, sex, and ethnicity) and psychographics (lifestyle)?

What can you offer your customers that your competition can't?

Do you have enough knowledge to succeed? If you don't, learn all you can about your product, and if you can, hire someone who has the experience and knowledge that will increase your chances for success.

Can you make enough money to meet your needs and wants?

Using a spreadsheet will give you an objective approach and give a good, dispassionate overview of your business. This is no time to get nervous or worried; try to remain unemotional and calm. (Make sure you write this all down—all the answers to the above questions) because it becomes part of your business plan and will help further define your strategies and tactics.

CHAPTER 4

School of Hard Knocks... the KOME Experience From Here to Infinity

In this Chapter:

- To not make my mistakes
- To be prepared
- To play from your strengths
- To write a short business plan
- That your failures are a necessary step to success
- To trust your own instincts
- To keep it to together when surrounded by "unusual" employees

After signing the April agreement to purchase KRPM, I returned to the San Jose market in August 1970 to do preliminary research. KRPM was a classical music station with meager billings, but it had a 50,000 watt signal that covered San Francisco to Monterey. The Station was a sleeping giant. In 1970, San Jose was the 29th largest radio metro with tremendous population growth. The city is 40 miles south of San Francisco. KRPM's signal blanketed most of counties in that legendary city's metro area.

The bay area was the country's center of counter-culture. San Jose was a city waiting to grow up. A decade later, it became the center of technology, maturing as Silicon Valley. In 1970 the area experienced growing pains, transferring from a small town mentality to a city beginning to become more sophisticated. It was an awkward phase for everyone. It was urban modern sprawl growing one strip mall, one car dealer at a time, franchise by franchise, with no identity of its own. And who was I to take root in such a place? The first thing I noticed was that there were a ton of pizza places and none had an Italian name—alien ethnicity.

I was a fish out of water. I came from the East Coast where I thought "laid back" meant returning the favor. I didn't do drugs, and here I would be surrounded by people whose life didn't exist without them. It was culture shock. I entered a different world, one I wasn't prepared for.

I moved to Los Gatos, at the foothills of the Santa Cruz Mountains, home to thousands of people with alternative lifestyles. At the very least they were an alternative to mine. I could tell you everything about the Fab Four or the Four Seasons, but I couldn't tell you the name of the four-fingered guitarist with the Grateful Dead. I appreciated the rebellion against restricted play lists but I wasn't prepared to adopt the anti-identity of free form radio. Like the Beatles said, "I should have known better."

Principle: Your chances are greater when you have substantial knowledge and love of your business product. The pants won't fit any better just because you lied to yourself about the size of your waist.

Though I had already made more money than many do in a lifetime, I was still young and inexperienced. When you have more to lose, the knocks seem harder to take in the school of hard knocks. But if you stay alert, the lessons can be more substantial. They say you learn from your mistakes. In that case, I deserve a PhD in Blunderology. I made more mistakes and learned more from the KOME experience than any other business. In hindsight I learned the trick is to remember that every time you fall on your face, at least you're moving forward. And whatever you do, keep going and tell yourself the truth learned from your errors. If every time you fall on your face you redouble your efforts to cover your ass, you're going nowhere. If you can't be true to yourself, who can you trust?

In 1970-71, FM was beginning its domination of radio. By the hundreds of thousands, listeners left AM for of the alternative sounds and quality of stereo FM. At the time San Jose had one Oldies station KLOK (AM). I wanted to compete with them, which would have been the right decision. I regret I never did. Less than a year later, KARA, another FM station in the market, switched to Oldies and had great success.

I would have been happier making KOME an Oldies station, but perhaps because I was a stranger in this strange land, I doubted my instincts. What passed for research back then showed audience dissatisfaction with KSJO-FM, a hard rock station that was number one with men 18-34 and had excellent billing. Most of the people interviewed who seemed most passionate about FM rock radio wanted an alternative to KSJO. It seemed at first glance that KSJO was vulnerable. At the time, I too was in the 18-34 demographic, and guys in that demographic group thought the entire universe revolved around "us."

But it was another mistake: my research was flawed. I interviewed more than 500 people, skewed to younger listeners— ignoring most people over 35. When you do research, hire a competent, research firm, or if you do it yourself, make sure your survey covers all the demographic (age) and psychographic (lifestyle) targets. Remember, research is only as good as the questions asked and how they're phrased.

Make sure to look at the whole picture before you begin to take the photo. Otherwise you might be cropping out some of the most important parts.

More than half the people interviewed wanted an alternative to KSJO. The people around me were lobbying to make the format hard rock. I got caught up in their passion and enthusiasm, went against my better instincts, and decided to make KOME a progressive rock station.

> **Principle: Get yourself a good trustworthy support group of businessmen and women and trusted friends. Surrounding yourself with sycophants, even if well-meaning and passionate, might make you feel good, but won't guarantee you'll do well.**

I had been a radio personality and didn't know the importance of a good business plan.

> **Principle: Make sure you have a well-developed business plan. If you can't do it yourself hire someone with a successful track record who can. Get a solid consultant, not just the lowest bidder. It's essential for your success.**

There are many good books on business plans and consultants. You don't need a business plan to succeed, but it can help. I prefer a shorter plan to a longer one. At the end of this chapter, I'll give you important questions to ask yourself that will help you on the road to your success.

I had always worked from my instincts and they had never let me down...until KOME. My instincts told me to do what I know: Oldies. Instead I became a stranger in a strange land of hippies, drugs and rock and roll.

As General Manager of KOME, my salary would be less than 20% of my teenage dances' income. My partner Mel bought a station in Maryland, where he lived, leaving me to run my first radio station alone. He had confidence that I, who had never run a radio station, could pull it off. He saw what I had accomplished at WIFI and had invested in KOME. He was only half right, as you'll see later.

Please remember this: if someone is successful in one area, it doesn't guarantee success in another (even if it seems tangentially related). When you make a decision to hire an employee, make sure that person is qualified to do the job you're hiring him to do. Give him plenty of room to aspire, but give him the support he'll need to stretch without snapping. I was neither prepared nor supported, at least not yet. I would learn the hard way. I never flinched from being the underdog, but taking on KSJO presented many problems, obstacles and challenges. I suppose you could say it was an "anti-establishment" station taking on a more "established" "anti-establishment" station. Going to the left of them made us too radical, while going to the right meant we wouldn't be "radical" enough. It's enough to make you pluck out all the flowers in your hair until you're bald and thorny. They also had a budget rumored to be $50,000 a month—four to five times my budget. I had invested all my savings into the station, which left me with little working capital.

How can you succeed against an established competitor with greater resources?

> **Principle: You think, think and think. You use all your brain cells. And when you hit yourself over the head later on, you do so with such compassion that you still have all your brain cells left after you do.**

How can you promote, position and start a buzz with little or no dollars? I started my attack with the call letters—KRPM. I had to come up with call letters that listeners wouldn't forget and would help build a brand. I decided to petition the FCC to change the call letters to KOME (come)—an exploitable double entendre. The FCC approved the call letters; after all, KOME was just a word. It wasn't even on the list of the FCC's seven banned expressions. The second move I made was hiring disc jockeys who were totally different from each other, and gave them a free hand to pick their own music, since they knew a lot more about the music than I did. Well, they might have known more about the music and the culture, but they were woefully inept when it came to taking that knowledge and translating it to the business, structure and programming of a successful radio station. Trying to turn these rag-tag hippies into a cohesive family was an impossible task—almost as difficult as the woman who marries a scoundrel thinking that the love of a good woman would change him forever.

> **Principle: Start your recipe with fresh ingredients— the best. If you can't afford decent help, maybe you should reconsider the mission. Don't enter the race with a lame horse and expect by some miracle that you'll win. Those are terrible odds.**

The air staff was an eclectic group and, except for my morning person, was a bunch of stoners. In the bay area in the early 70's drug use was rampant, especially in 18-34 adults (I use the term "adults" loosely). The staff was not allowed to use or bring any drugs into the station. That didn't stop some of them (and their colorful parade of friends and visitors) from getting high before they arrived. They were all talented and good people, with one exception, who definitely inhaled and was quickly fired. I loved the staff at KOME and the new challenges they presented to me. I was determined to give the station an identity, with jocks who were different and free to present their own style and music.

Cliff Feldman, sales person, and later the Program Director, wrote after a 2006 KOME reunion: *"Hey! Let's give some due to the original KOMErs...the ones who had no money, no corporate suits, and did I say, no money? We DID have far more creativity than the Infinity types who followed. Where else could you hear Sun Ra, Bobby Womack, Man, wicked cool segues and a real astrology show...all within a few minutes of each other? (Answer: nowhere). Of the original KOME staff, a number of us 'survive'. Present and accounted for were original owner Ron Cutler, original air staff Gary Torresani (currently a social worker), Uncle Jack (Tossman), Michael 'Mother' Deal, and 'Wapaho Joe' Amadeo, a 17-year-old-kid, who started his career at the station; also present was first sales manager Dick Bartholomew, myself (Cliff Feldman—hired as salesman and became Program Director in 1974 under second General Manager Dan Tapson), and the Lovely Linda (Caminada, or Burriesci), the station's first receptionist.*

Those were the days my friend, when radio was about the true personality of each jock and the music they loved. It wasn't about play lists or corporations. No insults, gags, or shock jocks; It was about a bunch of people who loved their music and loved to share it.

KOME was a legendary station, and it helped me continue down the road to success. If nothing else, I made it possible for a number of people to prolong their adolescence far beyond its traditional expiration date.

Now that the programming was set (product), next came building the station's awareness in the marketplace. We created an attention-getting car decal—the KOME sticker with its bold black and yellow colors. In less than three months, more than 20,000 cars had them on their bumpers or windshields.

> **Principle: Make sure the product or service is up to snuff before your marketing blitz. The worst thing you can do is to draw attention to yourself when you're not ready for prime time. So many entrepreneurs are whizzes at marketing but simply don't know how to deliver a product. Too much sizzle for too little steak isn't well done. It's burnt out.**

I decided to move the KOME studios from a small shopping center into the prestigious Prune Yard Towers, an office building in the back of a large regional shopping and entertainment center. We were on the thirteenth floor and our studios and offices overlooked the entire Santa Clara Valley. But I overlooked more than that. I paid too much rent, didn't have enough space, and the image we portrayed at that location was the wrong one. You'd think I'd have seen the parallel from the experience I had in choosing locations for my record hops.

> **Principle: Look for the lessons from parallels in your previous ventures. Once you see a pattern in your decisions, you'll be able to catch a potential mistake and redirect your efforts. Our bad habits only remain hidden if we choose to ignore the consequences of them.**

On the Road to Success:

As I stated earlier, you don't need a formal business plan to succeed, but you must ask yourself the following questions. Make sure you write down your answers and solutions.

Describe your business, product and service.

Is there a market for your product or service?

Who is your competition?

What advantages will you offer your customer that your competition doesn't?

What benefits do you offer your customers?

What's your unique selling proposition? It's what makes your business unique and gives you advantages over your competition, and gives more features and benefits to your customers. Nowadays, people use the term "product (or service) differentiators," but just because you've got something different, it doesn't necessarily make it more valuable to your customers. Also, when you see multi-syllabic words like "differentiators" in business books, beware of "corporate speak." If you can articulate your business plan in simple language, it probably means it's less complicated to carry out.

How will you promote and market your business? Remember the four P's of marketing: product, people, pricing and promotion.

Who are your targeted customers or clients?

How much money will you need to start and sustain your business for at least the first year? Respect the possible downside. How will you know when it's time to throw in the towel before wishful thinking replaces pragmatic optimism and you find yourself in a hole of your own digging?

Make sure you have enough money. Most businesses fail because they are undercapitalized.

Write down your operation and management plan.

Hire a good attorney and a good accountant.

I learned the hard way the solutions to the above questions. I would never do another business venture without answering them first.

CHAPTER 5

KOME (Continued—The Agony and the Ecstasy)

In this Chapter:

- How to get the most out of your promotion dollar.
- How not to panic in a crisis.
- How to deal with one crisis after another.
- How to avoid having your legs broken.
- How to be prepared for your worst nightmare.
- And more on branding and positioning.

Principle: If you look at promotional dollars not as expense but as investment, then you'll have a better way to measure the return on your investment and probably spend less in the process.

I positioned KOME as the hipper, cooler station that featured different personalities, a wider selection of music and an unusual presentation and format. The assumption here was that hipper, cooler and unusual would translate into "better", and with more benefits to the customer. Now that I'm older I realize that hipper, cooler and unusual aren't always better. As nice as it is to be an agent of change, in the marketplace change has its own timetable. If you're there when it happens and not too soon or too late, you're golden.

I wanted to brand KOME with station ID's that sizzled, were funny and generated a buzz in the market. I created an ID that had the whole market talking. I hired a sexy-voiced female announcer who said, "Doctor...doctor...I don't know what's wrong with me, I turn on 98.5 FM and I can't stop coming." It was clean if your head wasn't in the gutter, but our target audience was men 18-34. In less than 48 hours, our listeners found us. ID's and promotions turned the market upside down and the station's audience began to explode. People were buzzing about KOME, the hot new station in the market with a wider selection of music and wild and crazy jocks. It was a cheap shot, but more importantly, it was a bull's-eye.

> **Principle: In communication and in promotion, it's not what you transmit—it's how it's received. In sales, the impact is in the customer's mind. The good salesperson doesn't sell to the customer. Rather, he gets the customer to sell to himself (and his friends). It's an inside job.**

I had a tiny promotion budget. I spent my promotion dollars on 25,000 KOME car decals; that were yellow and black, with a large arrow pointing up toward the sky and in giant letters

KOME

and 200 thirty-by-forty-inch posters, placed in strategic locations around the market. Unlike the densely populated areas of Philly, San Jose was more spread out, so each location was even more strategic. The car decals and posters cost the station less than $2,000. I had our station sponsor a concert at the Santa

Clara fairgrounds featuring Savoy Brown, Joe Cocker and Rod Stewart. A capacity audience of 6,000 attended. My jocks were supposed to emcee, but most of them were too shy or not available. Still, the Santa Clara concert promotion didn't cost us a penny. In fact, we made money from the concert promoter's advertising. The event happened seven weeks after we went on the air and helped build station awareness and image.

> **Principle: Leverage your promotional dollars. Take advantage of all cooperative advertising and pick partners who share your goals. When two or more partners are gathered in the name of marketing, miracles can occur.**

We attracted small advertisers with even smaller budgets. We were positioned as the counter-culture station, a mistake because half our audience wasn't. I hired a couple of sales people who did the best they could. My biggest mistake was hiring a new national advertising rep firm based in New York whose specialty was hard rock stations. Hard was the right word, because it was hard for them to sell national and regional advertisers. That rep firm was out of business in a few years. When KOME was later sold to Infinity, it became their first station they purchased. Years later, Infinity became the largest owner of FM stations in America. The new owners hired the right firm and national and regional sales skyrocketed—many, many times the dollars that my old rep had sold. Interestingly, the new owners had the same size audience I had worked my butt off to attract. If we had had a better national and regional advertising rep firm, the station never would have been sold. Our local sales were fair, but without any measurable regional or national advertisers we had no chance of being profitable. Our local sales almost broke us even, but with national and regional sales at under $1000 a month, we didn't stand a chance of being in the black. I had a few good sales people, but some were stolen by rival stations with better offers. Our biggest source of revenue was from record companies. Every Friday I would journey to San Francisco, where the labels had set up regional offices, to sell them spot buys. Local sales came from businesses targeting the counter-culture: record stores, head shops, concerts, restaurants, bookstores, night clubs, etc.

Your target audience is a moving target. Be focused, but also be flexible. You'll succeed when you hit the bulls-eye, but you'll flourish by consistently hitting the whole target. You'll expand your opportunities around the edges. Use your business to create community. It may be one of the best investments you'll ever make. Even in today's online "virtual" business world, companies like Amazon, Facebook, Twitter, and Linked-In have built communities around common interests. Back in the '70s we did it in person. Your customers do need an invitation to get to know you and one another and, in KOME's case, their advertisers.

Bizarre Bazaar was created by KOME as an audience promotion created to stimulate ad sales. KOME rented the Santa Clara fairgrounds. All our advertisers were invited to have booths. Local bands played. The event turned into a mini-Renaissance fair. It was a success—over 10,000 people came, generating a terrific response both in sales and station awareness.

But it was difficult running KOME. With my lack of experience, the job was made even harder by some of the air staff. Over-developed egos with underdeveloped social skills makes for, if nothing else, an "interesting" workplace. At times, I felt I was running a nursery school. Although we had a singular mission to beat the competition and develop dedicated followers of our fashion, we were one big, often dysfunctional, family. By default and through unintended consequences, I was the patriarch. It was "Big Love" in the era of free love.

> **Principle: All business is family business. It's human nature to want to be taken care of. Loyalty is a two-way street. Employees always bring their "family of origin" issues into the workplace at some level. Parenthood's a bitch.**

I missed performing and so I created an opportunity to do an oldies show on KOME on Saturday afternoons. I started doing it and had a great time. I was Ron Diamond again (the first time in more than a year) and played the oldies. I was shocked by the response from our rock audience. Listeners would come by and dance in the studio, and dedications and requests poured in. After a few weeks, the show took-off; unfortunately that wasn't the only thing. On the third week of my show, a listener named Oren, wearing blue overalls and looking like he had stepped out of an underground comic book, appeared at the studio. He had an angelic face, blond hair half-way down his back, a long beard that came down to his chest and a devilish smile. He said he loved the show. He danced around the studio with a group of his friends. The next week, Oren returned with a chocolate cake. "It's a gift," he said. "I love your music and wanted to show my appreciation." The cake looked delicious and had a tempting smell. I was hesitant to eat it, but everyone around me convinced me to take a slice. Within five minutes, I had the microphone on the floor and couldn't stop laughing. For the next thirty minutes, all the listeners heard, was me laughing. Many called and said it was the funniest show they had ever heard. I ended the show and became my first fired Disc Jockey—ending my career as a radio jock. It would be 25 years before I would do another show.

> **Principle: If you can't do a particular job, fire yourself and give it to someone who can.**

Running KOME was always a challenge. Earlier I mentioned one of the biggest mistakes I made, choosing the Prune Yard Towers as our first studio and offices. Our listeners would come to our station with community service announcements and special requests. The management of the building with its staid business tenants wasn't thrilled that our station attracted flower children.

> **Principle: Don't try doing business in a place where you're not welcome... unless you're Wal-Mart.**

One day, a woman who looked like she had fallen off Ken Kesey's bus stopped by and asked to use the restroom. When she discovered there wasn't any Tampax, she wrote on the wall with bright red lipstick in large letters, "free Tampax for the sisters." The next day I was asked to come down to the building manager's office. He said, "If you don't move in a month...I'll see that both your legs are broken." A month later we moved into a mansion on the Alameda. No neighbor problems. We had the entire first floor and our neighbors on the second floor worked for an entertainment company. A steady stream of attractive people went up the stairs. They were quiet and never bothered us. They were rumored to be in the porno business.

> **Principle: Beware of landlords with no sense of humor and a baseball bat.**

March 21, 1971

I told you earlier about the concert KOME promoted at the Santa Clara fairgrounds. My jocks were scheduled to MC. A few of them were in no condition to perform, and others preferred to remain in the audience. I had hosted teenage dances and had no choice but to emcee the concert. A capacity crowd of 6000 people were there including my wife at the time, Judy, who was pregnant and due to deliver at any moment. I introduced the first act, Savoy Brown, then Joe Cocker and finally Rod Stewart. As Rod started rocking out, Judy's water broke and she went into labor. A few hours later, my first son, Jason, was born. He loves to dance, rock and sing off-key, but he's one great entertainer. I'm convinced that when Jason heard Rod's singing, he decided to make an appearance and became the final act that night.

> **Principle: No matter whom you hire, be prepared to step in and do their job at any moment.**

There were many serious challenges I had to face at KOME. One day, someone blew up our broadcast tower. The culprits were never apprehended. There were many possible suspects— a far-right wing group, a disgruntled listener, a fired employee or someone who was determined to put us out of business. Nothing would stop me from solving the problem and getting the station back on the air.

I called my air staff together. Our mid-day personality, Uncle Jack, was headed to his boat in Santa Cruz. He stopped everything and agreed to report to the station immediately. He wasn't the only one, the entire staff showed up.

I was calm under fire. I told them that each one had to man the phone lines and talk to callers. Listeners would tune in, not hear the station and might panic or want to know what happened. Hundreds called. The jocks were the station's link to our audience and even though we were off the air, we still were able to communicate with many listeners. I rushed to solve the antenna problem and get the station back on the air. My engineer,

John Higdon, immediately ordered the parts we needed and worked tirelessly. Miraculously KOME returned to the airways. Thanks to the air staff and John, the problem was solved in less than 24 hours. (It could have taken us more than a week to get back on the air.) The station was now more popular than ever. Whoever had tried to silence our station failed because now we had a stronger voice. Uncle Jack later told me that using the jocks to answer phones, and the calmness and determination I showed, became one of his greatest lessons. As I think about it, this problem wasn't that far removed from when certain people wanted to close down one of my dances. It was just on a greater scale.

> **Principle: When an unexpected crisis happens, know your priorities, stay calm, don't panic and make every effort to solve the problem as quickly as possible.**

Crises happen, but panic can be avoided. Focus on the solution and not the pain of the problem. Focus on customer needs first and foremost. Be calm, but more important, be competent. Use the jolt of energy that comes available in any crisis and use it where it can do the greatest good for the most customers in the quickest time. You'll be amazed at what you (and your crew) can really accomplish.

We Rattle the FCC

Our station served our community. We did many public service announcements. One of them, done by Uncle Jack, rattled the FCC. A few of our listeners became sick from bad acid they had purchased. Trust me, Alka Seltzer wasn't the answer. Uncle Jack read from the Redeye, the local alternative newspaper. *The acid is brown and yellowish and sells for $15. It's dangerous. Don't buy the stuff, it will get you sick.* In response a listener from Concord, in the East Bay, had written a letter to the FCC. A month later, I received a letter from the FCC accusing the station of selling drugs on the air. I wrote back and told them exactly what happened. After several months I heard from them again telling me that their investigation showed that we weren't selling drugs.

Running your own business is psychedelic. You'll need to expand your mind with novel creative ideas, stay open to what's in front of you and even the hidden dimensions... prepare to be wowed. And avoid the bad acid—the crazy advice from the well-meaning nuts and predators along the way. One bad freak-out can ruin your day. The ultimate business trip is day-by-day reality. It's best to get high on your success.

I have shared with you many of the mistakes made while running KOME. I can laugh at them now (and hope you have too) only because I chose to learn from them and bounce back, rather than see myself as a victim of such failures. It's not the failure that stops you from succeeding—it's what you do with it.

I did succeed in creating a ratings monster—number one in several demographics. I was limited by a small operating budget and overwhelmed with responsibility. I had to confront the reality of selling the station. Mel Gollub wanted out. I was fried. At the time, the FCC had a three-year rule that stated you could not sell a station at a profit unless you held it for three years. We had the station for 26 months. I knew it was worth four times what we paid for it, but under the rules we could only sell it for what we paid, plus any station's losses and improvements. Damn that FCC (can you say "Damn" on the air today?).

I knew whoever bought the station would have a goldmine. But I was exhausted. KOME, built with my blood, sweat and tears, would make someone else rich. I had my degree in hard knocks and never again would any of my efforts be wasted. KOME was my business degree. In retrospect, what I learned and experienced would serve me well the rest of my business life, as you'll soon find out.

Indirectly I helped to found Infinity Broadcasting, a company that would become the largest FM owner in America. A group of smart New Yorkers saw the KOME opportunity and pounced on it. Three brilliant and experienced people bought the station for around $400,000 (it was worth over a million.) It became the first Infinity station and because of the money, resources and talent they could bring to KOME they were able to build a radio empire on the profits from that first station, KOME.

Mel Karmazin joined Infinity in the early eighties, years after I sold KOME. Infinity became CBS radio and Mel became CEO at CBS corporate and Viacom, and now heads up Sirius Satellite. Our paths will cross in a later chapter.

On the Road to Success:

In this chapter you read some of my marketing techniques. Now, I'd like to share with you a few marketing ideas you might want to use if you have a small business.

Make sure you have a web site (this is essential for any type of business). It's a chance to know your customers, tell your business story and build a community (Even a small business should do this).

Most small business (retail, etc.) attract most of their customers within a 5 mile radius of their location, unless they're in a mall or a location with heavy traffic.

Below are several marketing ideas you might want to use:

- Direct mail targeted directly to your prime local area (this can be costly, but can be effective). Make sure you use an enticing offer (example: free gift or a deep discount on selected items).

- Use direct mail coupons, or if you want a less expensive way, have your coupons sent by companies like Money Mailer.

- Advertise in your local newspaper (the one that serves your community).

- Tie in an event at your store, restaurant, etc. with an organization, charity or one of your vendors, than spread the word through some of the above methods.

- Put posters and fliers around your target area. It's a cheap way to get the word out about your business and your promotions. (I've used this, and it's been worth every cent that it cost).

When you spend money on advertising or promotions, which is part of marketing, always measure your ROI (Return On your Investment). This is best way to measure the effectiveness of promotion and advertising campaigns.

Every time a customer comes into your store, ask them for their e-mail address. Tell the customers the reason is to give them advance notice of sales or special offers. Don't push them to give you their e-mail. Make sure you tell them what's in it for them (benefits, and make sure to follow up with benefits and build your community).

Make sure your vendors kick in co-op dollars if available (that's when they supply part or all of your advertising cost).

There are many more marketing ideas I'd like to share with you on my web site www.RonCutlerBooks.com and they are free.

CHAPTER 6

Thinking Outside the Box

In this Chapter:

- To think creatively
- To take a low risk with a high reward
- To get the most bang for the buck
- To get started with a small investment
- To learn more about decision-making
- To turn a loser into a winner

1972

I struggled financially; my income from KOME barely paid my bills. I had to find a way to supplement it. I began to look at all possibilities. The station had a large, dedicated audience. How could I use this to the station and my advantage? Then, suddenly, an opportunity appeared.

Fox Theatre, built in 1927, and a former Vaudeville house, now (1972) a shut-down movie theater in downtown San Jose, came up for lease. The theater had a 1700-seats and a huge lobby, the size of many theaters today. For first and last month's rent, I could get the lease of a fully-equipped film house in run-down condition.

> **Principle: When opportunity knocks and you think you can succeed, take it.**

The risk/reward ratio was excellent. I was risking $5,000 to make many times more than that. I took the deal and the next problem was my product. I looked for first-run and even second-run films, but none were available to me. At the time, one theater chain owned all the movie theaters in the San Jose market, making it impossible for an independent theater, especially one that had been closed, to book current movies. Now I had this 1700-seat movie theatre and no product. What do you do? You begin to think outside the box. You look at all your options. I had a large theatre with an enormous lobby.

Decision: I decided on running a repertoire film house. Instead of paying 50% of the film's gross to the film distributor (industry standard), I could rent films for $25 to $50 each. I would show movies like *Woodstock, Monterey Pop, Marx Brothers*, and *Harold and Maude*. But showing classic and cult films weren't enough; I needed to add more exciting features and elements. I converted the large front lobby into a mini-Renaissance Fair with fire eaters, jugglers and, in addition to the usual theatre refreshments, added healthy snacks and exotic coffees (unique at the time).

But I still wasn't done. I played two films on Friday and Saturday, and in between them I put on a local rock band. We had great local bands, one of which was the Doobie Brothers. My targeted market was the KOME audience. The product I was offering was exactly what they would respond to. We packed the Fox every Friday and Saturday and the "exhaust" wafting from the theatre got people high a block away. I got high on entertaining people and on the dollars I made. That kept me sober.

There are important lessons here:

If your plan for success becomes fixated on a single solution and it seems to be an impossible situation, you've boxed yourself in. Refuse the (self-imposed) verdict, surrender your brilliant plan and think outside the box. Embrace the opportunity hidden in every obstacle. Never give up. Don't expect your first solution to be the only right one; make sure you have at least four others. Then pick the best one; often it's the one that offers the least resistance. Go with the flow.

In the fall of 1973, KOME was being sold to Infinity Broadcasting (their first station), and at the same time I received an offer to sell the Fox. I decided it was good time to sell the theater and accepted the offer, made a huge profit, and moved on to my next challenge.

I wanted to move to Southern California, the place I dreamed of living since I was a child. On most New Year's days, Philly was frigid. I'd turn the TV on and watched the Rose Bowl game. The weather was sunny and warm and I promised myself someday I would live there.

In April 1974 I moved to Studio City in Los Angeles and my dream came true.

I arrived in Los Angeles, not sure how I'd make a living. Since I was 7 years old, I wanted to be a doctor, specifically a dermatologist. We lived next door to Dr. Manstein. When I was 9, he gave me a book on dermatology featuring rare skin diseases (leprosy and other exotic skin diseases) and after studying the sickening pictures I decided dermatology wasn't for me, but I still wanted to be a doctor.

It was May, 1974, I had some savings put away, but I was too old for Medical school and wouldn't get in anyway (no college degree). So I compromised with myself and decided to go to Chiropractic school. I spent a year there, got good grades, but decided I didn't love it (didn't like being around sick people all the time) and made a decision to go back to what I liked: entertaining people.

Principle: Life's too short; the easiest path to success is doing what you love.

At certain times in your life, you take stock and examine the thread that runs through your best times and greatest successes. It's a way to discover (through your past choices) more about your true nature and how it informs your life's purpose. For me, I enjoyed providing people with places to go that gave them a good time.

In February 1975, I had separated from my first wife, Judy, we had grown apart. In December 1975, I bought a house in the Westwood section of Los Angeles. I lived there for the next 16 years. A few weeks after I had moved to Westwood, Judy decided she needed a break, and left my 2 year-old son Seth and my 4-year-old son Jason, to live with me. It presented a new challenge (now I knew how working women felt), I had two small sons, meager savings and had to make a living, and still be a father 24/7. I decided to look for a business I would enjoy owning, and when I did, I would hopefully be able to hire a nanny for my sons when I was working.

1975

THE DISCO ERA
(STAYIN' ALIVE ISN'T ENOUGH. YOU SHOULD BE DANCIN'...YEA)

Disco was just beginning to take off. My record hop experience would come in handy, but I didn't know the bar business. I looked around for a location that would be a low risk but high reward situation. I found a run-down Polynesian bar and restaurant a mile outside the trendy Marina Del Rey area. It had parking for four cars and previously had four owners in the last two years. All failed.

Decision time:

The location near Marina Del Rey had a legal capacity of 300. *(Decent size)*

The previous owners knew little about marketing and weren't good operators. *(Opportunity)*

There was one Disco in LA at the time and that was gay. *(No competition)*

I didn't have knowledge of running a bar or night club, so I hired Dino, who was a popular bartender at Brennan's, a bar less than a mile away.

Principle: When you're thirsty for knowledge, hire someone who can fill your glass with expertise.

The place had to be remodeled and I had less than $25,000 to work with.

The bar had rotted bamboo, so I sprayed it white and began to make the place look like Rick's bar in Casablanca. I found a hungry, competent designer and a well-referenced remodeling company that needed work and I hired them (note: make sure you don't go over budget).

I put in a Bose sound system, built a large dance floor and a u-shaped bar, perfect for meeting people (product –providing customers with an easy place to mingle and meet other people, and great music and a large dance floor for customers to dance their asses off, plus a comfortable ambiance, attractive waitresses and handsome bartenders. Add to that mix, aggressive creative marketing and virtually no competition, and you become like a Las Vegas Casino: the odds of success are in your favor.

> **Principle: Good design means form follows function. Don't let good looks overlook good design (even in your flashiest disco outfit).**

I hired an outside security company, which provided bouncers (essential if you run a night club).

Still I had a lousy location with inadequate parking, but there was good street parking nearby. But the location presented a major problem: it was a mile away from where the big restaurants and clubs were, away from the action. I needed to market the club extensively and as cheaply as possible. I knew that most clubs usually only had two busy nights, Friday and Saturday. I decided to have special attractions Tuesday thru Thursday, which created five potentially busy nights.

I arranged promotions with Jocks at KHJ, one of the leading Top 40 stations in the market, plus jocks from other stations as my Tuesday and Wednesday attractions. Thursday was Ladies Night and Friday and Saturday would be initially promoted on the radio to start the weekend momentum. To answer the glaring need for an after-hours club we stayed open additionally from 2am to 4am on Friday and Saturday nights (though no alcohol served). This also added revenues.

> **Principle: If you find a need make sure you fill it, and the dollars will roll in.**

I named the club Bahama Mama's after a song I used to play on the radio. Our specialty drink was named Bahama Mama and was a big seller.

The promotion and marketing worked. The place looked like I spent over $100,000 in remodeling. One way to be on the road to make a million bucks is to look like a million bucks without spending it. Unless it's your wife you're trying to impress, a big Zircon is as good as a Diamond.

Result: The club was crowded five nights a week. On Friday and Saturday nights Bahama Mama's drew between 800 and 1000 customers and the other nights, 400 to 600 partied and had a great time.

But after a year, I realized the lifespan of a night club is short-lived (most night clubs have a strong first year and then business begins to fall off), so I was able to sell the club for triple what I had invested. The buyers insisted as part of the deal that I create a major new club for them the largest in LA. So my new challenge was to create a second club, one that would set a new standard and become the biggest club in Los Angeles.

If a challenge excites you, go for it. Starting a business is like starting a family. Every trend has a cycle. You'll increase your chances for success by continually monitoring the temperature. Go for it just before it gets hot and stay with it. Staying in business is like raising a child. If you're paying attention, you'll know when it's time to let go and enjoy your success.

As you probably noticed by now, I'm moving in and out of businesses. The reason is simple: when a business is hot, that's when you sell it. If you wait till it cools off, you'll be lucky to get half of the dollars you sold it for when it was hot. The reason I sold the theater in San Jose was to be able to move to Southern California. The reason I sold Bahama Mama's was the roller coaster night club business cycle. If you were buying strictly a restaurant or bar, they normally have a longer life cycle than a night club.

My business philosophy probably began in late 1960. Not having heat and hot water for the two months in Philly during December 1960 and January 1961 had a dramatic influence on the rest of my life. It left me with a feeling of financial insecurity, which still haunts me. That's the negative. The positive? It gave me a burning desire to succeed so I love challenges. I love taking on the hard ones. I try to climb high mountains, falling off sometimes, but other times reaching the top. I'm competitive, more with myself than with competitors. I'm an average guy with average intelligence but always pushing my limitations and in a constant battle to improve myself. And if I can do it, so can you.

I love challenges—that's why every business in this book is either a start-up or turn-around. When I buy a business, I have certain goals and when they're met, I make a decision whether to hold on or sell them. I did the Ron Diamond Dances for eight years and *Cutler Productions* for nearly 17 years; these were businesses I wanted to build. I loved doing Ron Diamond. When I got tired of being a big fish in a small pond, and didn't like being a radio personality, I made the decision to stop doing him. Cutler Productions was a different story, as you'll see later in the book, when I built a business for the long term.

The Birth of Dillon's
1976

My first quest: look for a location for a major club. The buyer of Bahama Mama's bought the club not only for the disco, but for me to create for them a super club. I didn't want to disappoint them. I always try to deliver more than I promise.

If you keep your personal vision a few steps ahead of your promises to others, you'll stand a greater chance of exceeding expectations by keeping your word. The bonus you grant yourself is that you always grow yourself in the process of growing your business. The success is then intrinsic as well as extrinsic, granting you the psychological capital to invest in your next venture and not burn out from the previous experience.

Creating and opening what the owners hoped would be the biggest night club in Los Angeles was a monumental task. But I had confidence that I could find a winning location and turn the club into a winner.

If you don't have confidence and a positive attitude for what you're attempting, why should anyone else? When you see yourself as a success and can feel it, you'll be self-motivated to be decisive and to take dynamic actions, providing a higher probability for success.

Always try to find the best location. In retailing and clubs and bars (and even on the internet) it's location...location... location.

I started my search not far from where I lived. Westwood Village at the time was the entertainment center for Los Angeles and the home of UCLA. In the 70's it was the hot spot for most of the Westside of Los Angeles. People would pack the streets, especially on Friday and Saturday nights.

I walked every block of the village, but no location stood out. There wasn't any retail space and the few restaurants available were too small and too expensive. Then I walked Gayley Avenue and noticed a large four-story building that had been a carpet store and warehouse. It had a for lease sign. I checked the place out. There was 5,000 square feet on each floor. To do a club the whole place had to be gutted, wall-to-wall.

Decision:

Positives:
- A great location.
- No competition.
- UCLA had thousands of college kids a heartbeat away.
- A huge space—20,000 square feet.
- Large parking lots nearby.
- At the time this was where all the big movie theatres were located, and most of the film premieres.

- The number of young adults that went through
  Westwood Village was staggering.

Negatives:

- Cost: at least one million dollars to turn the warehouse
  into a club.
- Getting the permits and licenses could be a problem.

Solutions:

- The owners had the money and were willing to spend it.
- Their lawyers got the licenses and permits.

Now what to do with the place?

My recommendations, based on what I had to work with, and the business projections for each floor, were:

First Floor: Restaurant

Second floor: Disco

Third floor: Live Music

Fourth Floor: Concerts, comedy and private parties

My partners at the time approved the plan and hired the interior design people who did Bahama Mama's. They also hired an experienced operator to run the restaurant.

I had 15% ownership but I couldn't devote myself full time. I had my two young sons, Jason and Seth, living with me. Instead I would work twenty hours a week and get a consultant fee for two years. For this, I gave up my 15%. In hindsight it was a bad business mistake, but a great personal choice. Family was all important and this allowed me to have the lifestyle I wanted and be with my kids more.

When a conflict pits business against family, any solution that doesn't allow you to win on both fronts is an unacceptable compromise. Even for Tony Soprano, business can be a seductive and ultimately lousy mistress. If there is any conflict between business and family I always put family first. I suggest you do the same. The true riches in life are your family as well as your friends.

I suggested we call the place Dillon's, a good name for that time and the owners loved it.

A large elevator that carried 75 people was installed in the center of the place, along with staircases to give easy access to each floor.

I wrote the operation manual. The owners hired Rogers and Cowan, a major Hollywood PR firm, to do the promotion. They were the best, but did they know how to promote and market a night club? Rogers and Cowan struck gold immediately by making the opening night of Dillon's the premiere party location for A Star is Born starring Barbra Streisand. A long red carpet ran from the Village Theater to Dillon's and many celebrities including Barbra walked it. The opening was a huge success. Rogers & Cowan had hit a homerun. After the opening, business didn't meet the owners' expectations.

The first two week grosses were disappointing and I got the call to take over the marketing and promotion. I started by getting area radio stations to promote Dillon's with some advertising and tie-in promotions on Tuesday and Wednesday nights. I then promoted on campus heavily at UCLA, placing ads that I knew would appeal to my target audience in the well-read UCLA daily newspaper The Daily Bruin. I started a buzz by going to fraternities and sororities (pushing Thursday night "Ladies' Night") and created incentives to UCLA students already going to Dillon's (free admission) to spread the word to the right people, which helped make word-of-mouth advertising explode.

The result was that within two weeks, Dillon's grosses increased 600 percent. Thursday, college night, we were at capacity and had to turn people away. Friday and Saturday nights were packed with over 2000 people. Business was great the two years I was with Dillon's. By then my contract was about to expire. My parenting situation with my sons had improved. That would allow me to work more than the 15-20 hours a week I did for Dillon's.

You don't have to be a genius to succeed in business. Learn all you can. Work hard and become an expert in as many things as you can about your business. Be it selling, marketing, product knowledge, or customer service. Whatever you love, be the best you can be, and make sure to hire good and experienced people in areas you need help, or, if that fails, get a franchise. Remember; be honest and responsible in all your dealings with customers, employees and vendors.

By the seat of my pants, the sweat of my brow and by not being intimidated to ask naïve questions to folks with greater experience, I acquired a decent amount of marketing knowledge and it paid off big for Dillon's.

Now, toward the end of my two-year commitment to Dillon's, I was looking for new mountains to climb and the best was still to come.

I decided I didn't want to continue in the night club business. I didn't like the late night hours, and besides, the night club business is short-lived. I wanted more stability and needed a business I could run for many years. I wanted to return to radio, which had always been both a love and passion.

So again my career would make a major turn, one which led to the kind of success I always wanted to achieve. I can't wait to share it with you.

On the Road to Success:

- Do what you love.
- Always measure your risk to reward when starting or buying a business.
- Be careful how you invest your money. Watch every dollar you spend. A dollar saved is usually worth twice as much as dollars you'll gain from gross revenues.

- Always look for a competitive advantage. (A feature or benefit your competition doesn't have or offer).
- Remember who your target audience or customers are, and make sure your marketing targets them.
- Before making a decision, be sure to write down the pros and cons. It leads to better decision-making.
- Think and be creative. Dare to be different and unique and your road to success will be faster.

CHAPTER 7

Return to Radio

1979

In this Chapter:

- How national radio shows were created, produced and developed.
- How I met a radio giant, one of America's greatest businessmen—Mel Karmazin.
- How I produced a show that featured Nobel Prize winners and the greatest thinkers of the time, like Buckminster Fuller and Ray Bradbury.
- How I made my first major national advertiser sale.
- And how I experienced failure and faced a dark future.

Six months had passed since I finished my Dillon's consulting job. I needed to get something started as my finances screamed that it was time to get back in action. I was fueled, energized, enthusiastic and ready for the next challenge to start something new. I looked at various entertainment opportunities, but one yelled out to me. I loved radio. I always did local radio, but now my eyes turned to national. Radio syndication and barter were in their infancy. I decided it was a good time to enter the fray. I would start a radio syndication company—creating, producing and developing radio programs or services for local radio stations across America. I would provide them with a program or service in exchange for commercials on their station and then sell those commercials to national advertisers, producing revenue.

I had no idea how the radio syndication business worked. At the time, radio barter syndication was relatively new. I studied the business and noticed it had three major components: the product (the show), station clearance (getting stations to carry the programs or services) and national advertising sales. I did analysis of the few companies in the business and interviewed people working in the industry. I talked to station relations sales people and did as much research as I could. I put together a business plan and presented it to an accountant who was looking for investments. He raised start-up money from private investors and I was ready to launch two programs.

I found a small office space on top of a Pizza Parlor on Westwood Boulevard and rented the second floor space. I hired a secretary, Jane, who would later work for Norman Pattiz, the head and founder of mega-syndicator Westwood One. I then hired three station clearance people. I went to New York and asked advertisers and agencies for recommendations of qualified potential ad sales reps. The buyer of Proctor and Gamble recommended someone. I interviewed him; he was likable and had a sales personality. But later I discovered I had made a mistake—I should have interviewed more candidates. The difference between a mediocre sales person and a great one: the ability to close the sale. Many sales persons are likeable, and even can give a good presentation, but for some reason they don't know how or are afraid of closing the sale (that's the ultimate goal). You'll never close 100%, but I learned the secret of closing before I was 20. My experience as a collector for the finance company (earlier in the book) and the Dale Carnegie Sales course, which I took when I was 19, helped me to become a good closer.

> **Principle: In business you make mistakes. No one is perfect, but the wise man learns from them and the fool keeps making the same mistake over and over.**

Going into radio syndication and programming was scary for me. I had no experience. So I did what I always do when I'm tackling something new: learn as much as I can. I talked to the few people in the field. I read the radio trade newspapers to get a feel for the business. I studied the few successful companies and tried to learn from and emulate them. I hired Larry Yurdin, who had some experience working for ABC Radio Networks. I looked at the programs out there and looked for holes to fill. Later, when I had more experience, I wasn't afraid to compete against companies many times the size of my company. When I did, I rarely lost in head-to-head competition. Was I lucky? Probably. Anyone who knows me will tell you I give 150% effort on everything I do, in business and in life. I'm no Gates, Zuckerberg or Jobs; just an average guy who gives it all I've got. Because I know I'm not gifted, I have to work harder than the competition. I never graduated college (about the only thing I have in common with the fore-mentioned geniuses), but I read voraciously (I have a library filled with 5,000 books).

What drives me? I want to be the best I can be. It does create a problem because I'm harder on myself, probably more than I should be. But I figure you have only one life, make the most of it.

Back to my first venture into radio syndication. The first show needed a producer who would have to be brilliant and a futurist. I found the answer in one of the most talented people I have ever known, Howard Cohen. He produced the show, and he and his assistant did most of the interviews featuring some of the greatest minds the world had ever known. Now everything was in place for the launch of the first show.

My first program was called *Future File*, a 90-second feature that interviewed the greatest futurists, including Nobel Prize winners and the greatest thinkers of the time, like Buckminster Fuller or Ray Bradbury. Howard and I worked closely on creating it (Howard became a close friend and, when he died in 1999, it was a gigantic loss for me. I miss his wit and genius).

The *creative process* for *Future File*:
You start out by asking yourself questions:
Question: What was the theme or idea behind the show?
Solution: The world's leading futurists, which included Nobel prize winners, would be the attraction.
Question: What would the format of the show be, how would it be executed and finally, what is the length of each show?
Answer: Howard and his assistant would do the interviews and the interviews would then be edited down to 90 seconds by our radio engineer. Next, a musical sound theme, which would lead into the show (10-15 seconds), and the sounder that would end the show (both had to be not only attention-grabbing, but also fit the theme of the show). Next was finding an announcer narrator. I was lucky; I found a exceptional announcer who could deliver the goods.

Question: Target Market
Answer: Men 18-34 (AOR Stations – Album Oriented Rock)
Question: Who would clear the show on radio stations?
Answer: Our new stations relations department
Question; Who would sell the show?
Answer: Our sales person in our New York office. I had rented an executive office at 42nd and Lexington when I hired him.

Future File was hosted by Dave McQueen who had one of those deep authorial voices. It was targeted for AOR (Album Oriented Rock radio stations), whose primary targeted market was men 18-34. When you do a syndicated radio show it's important to clear as many stations as possible, particularly in the Top Twenty markets. It's essential to have New York, Los Angeles and Chicago. Most national advertisers wanted at least two of these markets and preferably all three. My station people were clearing most of the AOR stations in the country, but we still needed New York. I flew to the Big Apple and met with Mel Karmazin, the crafty General Manager, who would later go on to run Infinity Broadcasting, CBS and Sirius. Mel was not only an excellent operations person but the greatest salesman I had ever known. I made a deal with Mel to run *Future File* on WNEW-FM.

My salesman put a great effort into selling the program, and had several advertisers interested, but had trouble closing them. Syndicated radio being new at the time wasn't an easy sell. One of the advertisers sitting on the fence was Datsun, now known as Nissan. They had close to a million dollars for network radio, and had NBC, CBS, ABC and Westwood One pitching them. I flew to New York and met with Tom, the media buyer and the Agency's Executive Account Manager for Datsun.

First, I established a rapport with the buyers. Next, I found out what Datsun's goals were for their advertising campaign and their target audience (men 18-34). I listened intently to what Tom said. I then presented how *Future File* would benefit Datsun and told Tom and the account manager the advantages that the show offered them against buying a bunch of spots on the radio networks. *Future File* hit their target audience perfectly (80% of the audience would be males 18-34) and it would give his client their own show and be heard on radio stations in excellent times. I was lucky again: I closed the account and got most of the company's whole network radio advertising account for the year 1980.

Disco was big in 1979. There were 107 Disco radio stations in America. I came up with the idea of doing a national disco show simply because there wasn't any. I called the show *Steppin' Out* and hired Peter Hartz, a bright guy who was familiar with the disco scene, to produce. I had Rachael Donahue, with an incredible sexy voice, as the host. The concept was to visit the hot discos from coast to coast and have their DJ's introduce songs. We also had popular disco artist interviews with most of them introducing their own songs. The music literally never stopped, as the beat ran under all interviews. The only time the songs ended was for commercials. The two-hour show had only three commercial breaks per hour, allowing for long music sets, vital to a dancing audience.

We had 106 of the 107 Disco radio stations in America carrying the show. The show started in the fourth quarter of 1979. For the first 13 weeks, the program ran without sponsors. My goal was to start selling advertising during the fourth quarter for advertising starting in January. Most national radio buys are sold in the fourth quarter of the prior year (1979) for the next year. They're called up-front sales. Sales for the following year (1980) were great; over $1,000,000 had been booked. The problem was that Disco began dying, and most of the radio stations changed their format. Steppin' Out had stepped out of vogue.

> **Principle: Don't base your business on a fad—it's likely to fizzle and so will you. If you see a fad, get in early to make a quick buck, know it won't last, and be prepared to pull the plug after you get your initial profits.**

Datsun renewed *Future File* for another year. But with the failure of *Steppin' Out* plus the start-up costs, my company closed. I was disappointed and upset that despite my best efforts I didn't produce the result I wanted. When I created Steppin' Out there was a large audience for it, a great station line-up, it was an entertaining show, plus we had many sponsors lined up for 1980. I learned never do to do a show based on a fad and I never did again.

Business can be a struggle and sometimes circumstances beyond your control invade your best laid plans with a surprise attack.

I decided to take a few months off to regain my spirit, and go over everything that happened. I took time to ruminate on my own mistakes and what I could learn from them, and the whole experience, so I wouldn't make them again. I was persistent and determined to get ready for the next challenge. I fell off the mountain when I was near the top. Now I had to rebound, but this time I had more experience and I vowed never to fail again.

On the Road to Success:

After a business failure, give yourself an honest "exit interview." Take some time to write down what you did right and particularly the mistakes you made. The biggest mistake you'll ever make is not to admit you made one. Don't assign blame when the assignment is to learn success from the lessons of failure. What if a mistake was simply another way of doing something? Take the whole experience into perspective. The biographies of billionaires are filled with failure and overcoming adversity.

CHAPTER 8

Starting on the Road to Millions

In this Chapter:

- How to Create a National Radio Show.
- How to find a need and fill it.
- How one of the most successful shows in the history of Top 40 was born.
- How I rebounded from failure.
- How to never give up.

Spring 1982

After my first journey into syndicated radio, I took six months off. My experience from the previous months had knocked me out, and I needed time to reflect. I had shrinking savings, two children to support and now I had no income (a little scary). Tired and a little burnt out, I still contemplated my next move. Following a setback, you must regain your energy, and when you're ready, come back like a hungry lion. I analyzed my experience, what I did right and what I did wrong. I spent hours and days thinking what I could do next, and what I wanted to do with the rest of my life.

I had given it my best shot, but circumstances beyond my control (Disco dying) invaded my plan. I did make mistakes and vowed never to repeat them. I was determined the next time to succeed and never to hop on a fad unless I started it.

Through all the uncertainty and insecurity in those six months, a magic moment happened: I met the love of my life, Lori. Prior to meeting her, for six years I dated a lot (recovering from my first marriage), but never wanted an ongoing relationship with any of the women I dated. Lori and I now have been together for 31 years. She's amazing and radiates happiness and sunshine during the good times and bad.

Rested, and with a slew of ideas, I was ready for action. I began to look at holes in the market or needs that weren't being met. My passion, energy and creative juices had returned; I was energized and ready for the next challenge.

> **Principle: Take time to reflect. Your image might look better in a new light. When you're down, maybe you need a rest before you get up again. The best part of the American dream is the waking up. And, with eyes wide open, move on.**

I always loved musicals, from Broadway and Hollywood. There had never been a national radio show featuring music from Broadway and Hollywood musicals. I read in USA Today that such music was the fourth most popular musical choice of Americans. Was I on to something that thousands of radio programmers were missing—hard to believe, yet worth exploring?

> **Principle: If there's an elephant in the room, and you're the only one who notices it, there's still an elephant in the room. One way to succeed in business is to find a need and fill it.**

I called the show *Musical*, the greatest hits from stage and screen. I hired Chuck Southcott as host. Chuck had the voice and perfect delivery for the show.

When you found Broadway music on your local radio, the station usually played all the music from one show, including the less popular songs. I decided to play the greatest hits, music that people were familiar with, applying the same successful principles used in Top 40, Country and AOR stations everywhere.

Derivative works (borrowing an idea and putting it in a different context) can become a great foundation for a new creation. Sometimes what works on one stage can be adapted and replicated on many others. There is value to new content packaged in a familiar form.

The show was three hours long with each segment building on a theme. One segment presented a Broadway or Hollywood musical and played the most popular songs from it. In between the music the listener was told the story, as well as inside information. There were interviews with major Hollywood and Broadway stars like Carol Channing, Ray Bolger (The Scarecrow in The Wizard of Oz), Gene Kelly, Donald O'Connor, Debbie Reynolds, June Allyson, etc. More than one hundred Broadway and Hollywood stars were interviewed. There was one interview segment each hour. I picked all the songs, themes and blocked the show. Blocking is when you plan the entire show on paper. You decide the features, music selection and elements of the show and then decide the time and place in the show when they'll be presented. You also determine when the commercial breaks run. I presented the show to Tom Rounds, who launched *American Top 40*, with the legendary Casey Kasem. Tom was the president of Watermark, which had been acquired by ABC Radio Networks. Tom loved the show and recommended it to ABC who gave it the go-ahead. Tom is one of my favorite people and his contribution to radio has been enormous. He recommended I hire a writer named Ken Cauthern to write the show.

Ken was a Texan with a heavy Texas drawl. He was talented, likeable and became a close friend. Watermark sold the show to radio stations, rather than barter it. Bartering turned out to be more profitable. Barter is when a radio show, program or service is given to a radio station in exchange for commercial spots, which producers or syndicators then sell to national advertisers.

Though I wasn't the syndicator of *Musical*, it felt great to be doing something I loved: producing. I was an independent contractor. The experience was a perfect bridge between what I had done and soon would be creating and doing, which in the future would affect thousands of radio stations coast-to-coast and entertain millions of listeners. At Watermark, I attended producer meetings with other talented producers. I absorbed every bit of knowledge and stored it into my memory for future action (make the most of every opportunity you have).

Musical was profitable, but apparently not profitable enough for the big network and a year later, ABC cut three shows—one of which was *Musical*. I had just come back from my honeymoon with my wife, Lori, and the next day went into Watermark and found myself unemployed—a great way to start a marriage,

It seemed like bad news, yet I was determined to turn the negative into a positive.

Principle: When the honeymoon's over, that's when the work begins. Every musical has more than one act and yours isn't over until you dance in the grand finale. Even Shakespeare eked out a business from tragedy.

I contacted Tom and asked if I could get the rights to *Musical*. ABC didn't care, they were through with it. I took back the rights to *Musical* for a song…a song called "zero".

I only had $15,000 to work with, which I used to convert my garage into two rooms, one an office, the other a small studio. If I needed more money, I would take a second mortgage on my home.

The first thing I did was change *Musical* from cash to barter. Barter was an easier sale to stations because they didn't have to reach into their wallets to pay for it. I didn't have the money to hire a station relations person, so I cleared stations myself. It was another valuable learning experience. I started with the *Musical* library of shows I had acquired from Watermark (this kept my producing costs near zero). I used the telephone in the office in my garage. I had to make it work, or I'd be in the toilet (highly motivated). I hammered the phone eight hours a day, targeting Beautiful Music, Middle-of -the Road and Nostalgia stations. Determined and enthusiastic, I wouldn't let myself fail. I sold to stations not only the features of *Musical*, but all the benefits that station gained by carrying the show: a strong weekend show with a potentially large audience, plus the sponsorship opportunities stations could offer to their advertisers as an added bonus. I even mailed sales brochures to help stations' sales people sell the show. It took me three months of eight-hour days to clear 100 stations. After that, I had to sell advertisers (much harder). I sold a few, but my station list had potential, brimming with a large audience of 35-64 people. I decided to make a deal with Westwood One. They had a large sales staff that could maximize the advertising dollars *Musical* offered. I still owned the show, but sold the rights to sell and distribute to Westwood. Now the foundation was laid for my future success.

> **Principle: If you have limited funds, prepare to do everything yourself—it's called sweat equity. If you're a one-man show, the only thing you have to back yourself up is the belief that you can succeed.**

I cleared over 100 stations, including WMCA in New York, KIIS-AM in Los Angeles, and WPEN in Philly. *Musical* was heard in the majority of stations in the top 50 and 100 markets.

At the same time this was going on I received a call from Wally Clark, the General Manager of KIIS-FM. He had heard that *Musical* was dropped and asked if I'd meet him at his office the following Thursday about ways he could help me with *Musical*. I was to find out later that wasn't the only reason for the meeting.

> **Principle: Take a meeting. There's a shorter distance between a handshake and signing a contract that way. And always return calls. It completes the circuit that can lead to flipping the switch.**

I had opportunities, but what I did with them would determine my success.

I had married Lori on July 30, 1983 and returned home on Tuesday, August 2nd—lost my job on August 3rd—received a call from Wally Clark on Thursday, August 4th, and obtained the rights to *Musical* on Friday, August 5th. What a week! I felt optimistic and jubilant. Everything began to fall in place. This time I felt I would soar and be unstoppable: Opportunities had dropped into my lap and I knew nothing would stop me from reaching my goals. I was on the launch pad, fueled and ready to blast off.

> **Principle: When bad things happen, don't cave in. That's the time to take dynamic action. Think positive. Figure potential solutions to your problem. After you have a few written down, think some more, and the chances are good you'll think yourself into a solution to the problem.**

Musical ran on KIIS-AM, the sister station to its FM, and had over 70,000 listeners per quarter-hour on its Sunday 10am to 1pm spot. Wally was impressed with the show and the way it was put together, the production, content and how smoothly it moved.

I arrived at KIIS-FM, which was in a tall building on Sunset Boulevard in Hollywood. I sat in Wally's office less than five minutes, when he came to the true purpose of our meeting: Rick Dees.

Rick was a phenomenon at the time with an astonishing ten rating on his morning show. Wally had been working with his program director, Jerry, his production manager, Don, and several others to put together a demo for Rick's national countdown Top 40 show. They did a few one-hour demos, but weren't satisfied with the results. Wally asked me to listen to the demo tape and meet with him on the following Monday with any ideas I might have.

I called my friend Don Goldberg, a true eccentric creative genius, and exchanged ideas with him. Don was an artist, exceptional writer and had the most creative engineering mind I've ever experienced. Don thought outside the box constantly. Don was perfect for working with me on creating pilots. He worked slowly and meticulously on every detail. I understood him and appreciated his awesome talents. I was usually a loner when I worked with my creative spirit, but I enjoyed creating ideas and brainstorming with Don. Some people are designed to work on a show every week. Don's talent, because of his need for perfection and his slow meticulous working style, was ideal to working on pilots, not on weekly shows. When it came to doing pilots, Don was the best. He worked with me creatively in all aspects of the *Dees Weekly Top 40* pilot and also several other pilots.

Monday arrived. I walked into Wally's office, and to my surprise, the room was crowded with people. Rick Dees, Jerry the PD, Don the Production Director, Conway, head of PR and Coz, KIIS-FM's sales manager and Wally's sole partner with Rick in the venture.

I showed them how I would produce the show. I formatted the program, put in new elements like *Dee Sleaze, Offbeat* and other elements, suggested other ideas and blocked and outlined the entire four-hour show. They had worked for weeks on a one -hour demo and now Wally asked me to do a full four-hour show in less than two weeks. He gave me a very low budget to work with, but that didn't stop me from turning out the best product I was capable of delivering.

I went to work immediately and brought in my friend Don, who worked well with me. Don was an excellent production person. He worked 24 hours straight in a makeshift studio I had in my house, even while my wife and I slept. Every split second of audio had to be edited and mixed just right. Don reminded me that, when doing pilots, they had to be perfect, because you only have one shot at selling the show. Of course there's no way a person can do 100 hours of work every week for a four hour show. Shortcuts and efficiencies would have to come once it was sold.

We had to create jingles, which were the toughest things to do with our tiny budget and limited facilities. (Later, thank goodness, Wally hired a professional jingle house). Somehow I finished blocking the show, putting in all the features, determining what elements of the Dees morning show could be used and

88

which were inappropriate for a national show. Don did a fantastic production job and was my right hand person through the entire production process. Rick recommended Louise Palanker, a young talented writer with a flair for comedy, to be the show's first writer. Louise was bright and easy to work with. I was leaving to go on my "honeymoon" in two weeks so Don and I worked around the clock. It paid off with a full show demo. I dropped the tapes off to Wally on my way out of town. One of Wally's associates cleared the stations. The demo show instantly cleared nine of the top 10 markets. The show was hot, and Dees was hotter. I built the *Rick Dees Weekly Top 40* around Rick to showcase his talents. He was a perfectionist and a collaborator with a creative mind and was the quintessential Top 40 air personality. The show was a huge success going on to make millions, thanks to the talents of Rick Dees.

I asked for a piece of the show before it was launched, but was told by Wally it wasn't available. I was married, had two children to support and needed the money. I was hired as an independent contractor, responsible for paying the writer and engineer on the show and I pocketed a thousand a week. Not great, but a start, and what a start it would be. Considering my contribution I was disappointed not getting a piece of the show's ownership. I didn't like it, but I realized I could use the show to my advantage to further my career, and it turned out to be the right decision. In the next 13 years all my goals and dreams were achieved. From that moment on in 1983 my income increased dramatically every year until, I sold my company in 1996.

> **Principle: In business the one who can walk from the deal first has the advantage. From now on I would have the advantage. Never again would I do a deal where I was at a disadvantage and never again would create a show that I didn't own (100%).**

On the Road to Success:

In business I always have a passion, a burning desire to succeed. I love what I do. I love the challenge and enjoy making business fun. It keeps me going when the going gets tough. Make sure you have these attributes; they will help you on the road to business success.

Many times you're faced with a challenging event or situation that is upsetting—don't panic. It's happened to me on many occasions. Relax-take time to think of the best solution, a moment of silence is important. Think of all the pros and cons before coming up with the best answer. Make sure you've looked at all the possibilities before taking action.

Creativity is a big part of my life. I'm always looking for needs that aren't being met or problems to solve. If you want to increase your creative thinking, here are a few suggestions that may help you.

Know that you have the ability to think outside the box—to find unique solutions—you can if you try. Relax, do some deep breathing, and make sure your mind is clear. Look around and think, what's something you want, but can't find in any existing product or service? Do you think others would want it too? If the answer is yes, you may have a product or service that potentially could be successful. Remember, this is the just the starting point. Go to the brief business plan in this book and answer the questions. After that, you'll have a better idea if your project is worth pursuing.

CHAPTER 9

Taking Off

1986

In this Chapter:

- How I meet Howard Stern before he became the King-of-All-Media.
- How I create a show for Cousin Brucie.
- How I make a "Fly Jock" soar.
- How I create a national radio show.
- How Love hits the airways.

I made *Musical* profitable by building up a saleable station line-up, which enabled me to license the show to Norm Pattiz and Westwood One. Norm was the greatest salesman in radio syndication history and became a multi-millionaire because of it.

> **Principle: Street smarts, critical thinking, and common sense will always trump book smarts.**

A good radio producer is someone who can surround himself with great talent. He (she) has to be creative, imaginative, constantly thinking outside the box, have passion and maintain enthusiasm. He must be patient, diplomatic and tactful when dealing with the host of the show. The producer must have respect and appreciation for everyone involved in the show, particularly with the star's ego. Give the host constructive criticism and let him or her think it was his or her own idea. The vast majority of radio personalities I worked with were a delight. I have pleasant memories of all of them.

> **Principle: when working with temperamental talent, sublimate your ego and you'll supplement your income.**

I was now on the road to success. Each year my income increased. I had a license fee from Westwood One, and money from the Dees show, but I was looking to build something bigger.

After the Dees show I promised myself I would own all the shows I produced, and with one exception, I did. I'd been the first producer of *The Weekly Top 40* and, after nearly two years, Rick and I parted ways.

When I left the show, I lost a stable income (little scary). Now I was running a ship in uncharted waters. Insecurity showed its face, and for a brief time, haunted me, a very brief time, because now I had confidence that I would no longer be dependent on anyone but myself for my income. I learned from the lessons I shared with you. I had the battle scars and mistakes. Now, with all that I had been through all those years, I was ready to succeed big time. Nothing was going to stop me. As usual I gave it 150% effort and several months later, I replaced that lost income and exceeded it by a substantial amount.

> **Principle: If you're not satisfied with the status quo, then do something about it.**

I created a new two-hour show called *That's Love*. The program was about romance, relationships, and, most of all, love songs. This was just before it became popular for radio stations to play love songs at night.

I moved my office from my garage to the entire second floor of a small office building on Westwood Boulevard, around the corner from my house. I did the rare thing in LA: walked to work. I was taking a risk with the new offices and building a new studio, but if I didn't take it, I had no chance of success. Risk is an essential part of business, when you take it, make sure the odds are in your favor.

That's Love was hosted by two radio personalities, Dick Summer and Madeline Vlasic. They were great together. The show had interviews, show jingles written by Alan O'Day (famous for *Uncover Angel* and writing the Righteous Brothers' big hit *Rock and Roll Heaven*). It had Vox Pops (interviews) featuring people on the street, a psychologist, interesting topics, polls, celebrities and played the best love songs. Don Goldberg and I created the elements and format of the show and Don put the demo together in the studio. *That's Love*'s demo was good enough for Norm at Westwood One to license it. I still owned the show (licensing a show means you still own all the show's rights, but you're giving the network rights to distribute and sell it to national advertisers, which allowed me to create and produce a show with minimal risk or none). This is one way to start a business and make a profit the first week you're in operation. I had a guaranteed licensing agreement that would pay all the shows costs, and make a large profit for my company. If Westwood One cancelled the program, all rights would revert back to me. I was starting again and building a foundation for my business. *That's Love* ran for around three years and, when Westwood terminated it, my company had revenues that had gone from a trickle to a gushing stream.

Ken Cauthern, who worked on *Musical*, wrote and produced

the weekly shows of *That's Love*. The show ran for several years (*Musical* ran from 1983 to 1987).

As the company began to grow, I couldn't spend time producing the weekly shows. I had a company to manage and even though I was still involved in the shows, I maintained a hands-on approach to all departments. I was driving the ship and there wasn't enough time to do everything I wanted. I would create all the new shows and services: the concept, format, blocking and features, and then produce the demo. I would next hire the producer and hire a writer (sometimes it was the producer). My responsibility was to keep creating and developing new shows and services and growing the business.

Whenever I started a new show, I produced the show alongside the person I trained to be the new producer. After 3-7 weeks had passed, when I knew they could do it, I stepped aside, but always listened to each show and passed on any suggestions that I had.

I love creating, but my mission now was also to build a company. Any new company in the early stages can fail. I had to watch every step. If I made a major mistake and couldn't correct it quickly, the company would go under. Business is like a good novel full of conflict and drama. Remember I was still working on a shoestring (always dangerous) and anything could happen.

Yet at this time the company was moving in the right direction.

Starting a business is a stressful time (be prepared) and can cause a lot of sleepless nights, but I love a challenge, and the bigger the challenge, the more invigorated I am. I've been vaccinated because of my experiences against many of the emotional distresses that owning and running a business can produce. In many ways, I'm a lone warrior, never having a mentor, teacher or guru to personally show me the way. Yet my success is still dependent on my staff.

I've always had deep respect for my employees. If you worked for me, you were entitled to be treated well, appreciated and compensated accordingly. I had a responsibility to them and if I screwed up, my people could lose their jobs. I ran my company like a family, and I was at the head. If anyone had a problem, (no matter what their position) they could come into my office and discuss it with me. I was lucky that the majority of my employees were talented and intelligent. I gave them the freedom to do their best and they delivered. In all the years I ran Cutler, I only let five people go. And when I did it, their self-esteem was my high priority. I would tell everyone that they resigned and I made sure they were compensated well.

I was on the road to success with many of the people I just wrote about including Ken and Peter, my chief engineer.

I may have not made much money from producing *The Weekly Top 40* show, but it did help propel me to the next level. I had built a reputation in the radio industry, particularly among the radio networks and radio personalities, because of *Musical, That's Love* and *The Weekly Top 40*. I was now on my own and had revenues coming in from *Musical* and . I used a percentage of my company profits to expand my business and develop new shows.

You probably are wondering by now how I taught myself to run a business. I had no teacher or guide or personal trainer. I believe it started when I was in the sixth grade. I put on a circus at a yard across from my parent's apartment. I spread the word that afternoon that everyone should come to the lot on Franklin Street to have a good time. At 4:00 100 kids showed up and I charged them each 5 cents. It was my first entrepreneur adventure and gave me the idea that someday I would like to own a business.

Poverty is a great motivator if you use it in the right way. Forget the free-loading (welfare etc.); it kills your self-esteem.

When I was 17 and didn't have any hot water or heat for two months that lit a fire in me. I swore I would never be in that condition again. So I began my business education, first by going to the library and reading every business book I could. When I started making a living, I began to buy business books and read them from cover to cover (something I still do). At 18 I took a Dale Carnegie sales course. I was the youngest in a class full of IBM and major company sales people. Every week we had competitions. I won more than a few of them. I observed everyone in the class and gleaned what I could from each of them. I read books about business people who had succeeded, and I decided I would try to emulate the ones I liked.

I asked many questions from people who ran businesses. I became friendly with Peter, who owned the Concord Roller Skating rink. At that time no rinks were doing birthday skating parties. I asked if I could try to book some and I did, and made some extra money when I was 15.

I have more than 500 business books in my library of 5000 books. When I was younger I read all the time, mostly non-fiction. So I basically am self-made.

If you can, go to a business college, or if you don't have the time and money, take a night class or attend a seminar in subjects you're interested in, but don't stop learning. Study the type of business you want to pursue. Read business magazines and newspapers and other business and motivational books.

Here's a summary of character traits that helped me succeed over the years. They should help you as well.
- I'm willing to give 150% in everything I do.
- I'm enthusiastic and have a burning desire to achieve my goals.
- I have my down moments, but overall I'm a positive thinker.
- I always challenge myself, sometimes falling on my ass, but quickly getting up.

- I don't let obstacles stop me.
- I never stop learning.
- I'm persistent.
- I think outside the box.
- I treat all people with respect and appreciate them.
- I constantly work on my observation skills.
- I work on being a better listener.
- I try to be humble (though unfortunately sometimes I fail).
- I love my family beyond words.
- I'm intense and driven.
- I'm resilient; I have a knack of getting up after I've been knocked down.
- I'm not afraid of taking a risk as long as I have looked at all the pros and cons.
- I'm determined to succeed.
- I have a competitive spirit, mainly with myself, rather than with others (pushing me to do the best I can be).
- I enjoy reading and watching educational videos.
- I concentrate and focus as much as I can.
- I am always pushing myself to my limits.

<u>Here's a good idea to remember:</u>

Don't put all your profits in your pocket—it's smarter to put a portion of them into building your business. If you don't, and your business becomes static or, worse, in trouble, you'll regret it. Putting a percentage of profits into building your business is insurance that will lessen the possibility of your business failing.

It was 1986; I started doing research and new show development. I began creating and working on demos for three shows. I always fronted the cost of developing my shows. Because of my earlier experiences, I would never again create or produce a show I didn't own the rights to. Don Goldberg, who had known me since my days at WIFI and had worked with me on concepts, creation and pilots of my shows over the years, had moved to New York to work for a major east coast syndicator (DIR). He was hired for his creative talent, but they never implemented any of his ideas. Not a good way to retain "creatives." Their loss, my gain. I lured him back and flew him in for a few weekends to help me bring my next set of shows from concept to creation.

I was beginning to become a hot commodity. I was getting calls from CBS and ABC Radio Networks, as well as some of the biggest-named radio personalities who wanted me to create and produce national radio shows for them. I got a call from Don Buckwald, Howard Stern's agent that Howard would be in Los Angeles and would like to meet with me. I met with Howard in his suite at the Universal Sheraton Hotel. He was a gentleman and a truly nice guy—a phenomenal talent. Howard was on WNBC in those days and hadn't yet been on any other radio stations. He wanted to do a three-hour national show on Saturday morning. He is one of the best interviewers. I was eager to work with him. I had many ideas for the show that would make a strong show even stronger. I told my station relationship people to call stations to find out what stations would carry Stern's show. The response was overwhelming; more than 72 stations in the Top 100 markets would run the show on their station if we produced it.

Radio syndication has three parts: the program, the stations that run it and the national advertisers who buy spots on it. You need all three to work to have a successful and profitable show. Here's how I made the decision whether or not to do a show:

1. Product (show): Stern was great and the show from a programming point of view couldn't miss.

2. Station Clearance: There was strong interest from stations if we were able to produce and distribute *The Howard Stern Show*. Result – can't miss.

3. National Advertisers: We had our advertising representa-

tive poll national advertisers to see if they would buy advertising on the show. We couldn't find one that would. Even then, Howard was considered too controversial. National advertisers were afraid of sponsoring a show that featured scatological humor. I guess they didn't watch some of the TV shows they sponsored.

So to my regret, I had to pass on the show.

DIR, a good syndication company in New York City, launched the national Howard Stern Show in 1987. The show lasted less than a year and died because of lack of support from national advertisers. I'd guess that DIR lost a lot of money.

A few years later, Howard launched his daily morning radio show nationally; it was a tremendous success and didn't need the advertising support from national advertisers to become one of the most profitable radio shows of all-time. Howard is a true radio legend. I enjoy listening to his show on Sirius, and wonder how I could make a good (expletive now undeleted) show even better. I guess we'll never know.

On to the shows I did develop in 1986, for debut in January 1987.

Oldies music was a big part of my life. I created the Oldies show, *Cruisin America* featuring another radio legend, Cousin Brucie. Bruce Morrow had a great voice and delivery and was a delight to work with. I worked on the demo with Don in the studio and Allen Goldblatt writer for many countdowns (he wrote for Casey Kasem, Dick Clark and Murray the K). I decided to name Janis Hahn, whom I had worked with at Watermark, the producer of the show. Janis is one of the best producers in the business. I created the show and sat in with Janis in the production of the show for the first few weeks, then handed it over to Janis. I was busy now overseeing all aspects of the business. All the shows that my company produced (except one) I created or co-created.

99

Bob Kipperman, the head of CBS Radio and Frank Murphy, the Program Director, had visited my offices and said they would be interested in having me develop music shows for their network. I liked these guys a lot. Cousin Brucie was on WCBS-FM in New York and there were other major Oldies stations at the time that were owned and operated by CBS. I sent the *Cruisin' America* show demo to Bob and Frank and they loved it. I licensed it to CBS and the program ran for six years.

The second show I had in development was *On the Move*, an urban music countdown show. Urban music (for those unfamiliar with the term, is Rhythm & Blues and soul music). This show's format was to countdown from 30 to 1 the biggest Urban songs of the week. Ken Cauthern, who produced , brought Tom Joyner to my attention. Because he was a disc jockey doing both mornings in Dallas and afternoons in Chicago, he was called the Fly Jock because of his daily plane commute. I listened to Tom's shows and loved what I heard. He was funny, communicative and had many interesting and enjoyable features on his morning show. Ken and I flew to Dallas and met with Tom. We decided to try to create a national three-hour show for him. We came up with the natural title for the show, *On the Move*. No one in radio flew as much as Tom. He finished his morning show in Dallas, then hopped a plane to Chicago and then, at night, flew back to Dallas. He did this Monday through Friday when we met him. He called himself the hardest working man in radio and he certainly was.

I went to work on the demo. I blocked the show first to get its flow and how, when and where to use the show's features and elements. Tom had so many good features on his morning show that I had to figure out which ones would play best nationally. Tom was as funny off the air as he was on the air. I flew Don in to help put together the demo in the studio from Ken's script. Tom liked it, but asked if we might do another version that he thought would do even better. We did both versions and sent them out to ten leading urban stations in the country for feedback. The original version won by a large margin. Joyner's talent was as a stellar on-air performer. I knew what makes a national show work differently than a great local show.

> **Principle: Powerful people may seem like they know everything, but what makes them powerful is that they work with people who have the knowledge they don't have.**

I sent the show demo to CBS, who were eager for a show that would appeal to African Americans. They licensed the show and I had my second show on the CBS Radio Network. The show ran for seven years and only ended when ABC paid Tom millions to do a national daily morning show. They paid handsomely to release Tom from his contract with me. Tom's ABC show was a big hit. It's nice to see that nice guys can still finish first.

So yes, on the one hand I still licensed shows to the networks. But I retained all the rights. The networks could not produce the shows without me. If they dropped a show, I could take it elsewhere. The networks paid substantial fees to Cutler and I covered all the costs of production and still made a nice profit. It was an ideal way for my company to do business. I had profits from the day the show was launched and still had time to produce other shows and services. My company produced shows, cleared stations and, through our sales reps, sold our commercial inventory for the shows and services we distributed. It was the best of all worlds, allowing us more dollars for research and development of new shows and services. It also reduced business risk.

> **Principle: Always find ways to maximize both revenues and profits with the least amount of risk.**

The third show in development was *Party America*. It was targeted as a weekend night show that visited radio stations and entertainment places around America. Jimmy Roberts, an engaging New York disc jockey, was the show's original host. Correspondents from around the country would do updates from their cities and introduce the songs. A year later, Jay Thomas, a talented radio and TV star, was added. The show ran on the ABC Radio Networks for two years. When they dropped it, my company syndicated the program for another four years.

Cutler Productions (the name of my company) expanded rapidly. In 1987, we were the only production and syndication company producing simultaneous programming for CBS, ABC and Westwood One Radio Networks. The dollars were rolling in.

> **Principle: Work hard, innovate, persevere and continue to lay the groundwork—there's an excellent chance you'll hit pay dirt.**

Success breeds success. The first win may be the hardest. The next few may come in rapid succession because investors expect that by betting on a winner, they can better manage their risk. If you can't replicate or franchise your product or service, look for a derivative you can leverage. Why recreate the wheel when you can modify the vehicle, slap a new logo on it and send it down a parallel road?

I still had my three network shows, one of which I would take over distributing the next year. *Cutler Productions* now had sizable cash reserves and excellent revenues from the network shows. From here on, all new shows and services, with the exception of the current network shows, would be sold and distributed by Cutler.

The reason for my decision: I wanted to control the future of *Cutler Productions* and maximize my revenues and profits.

On the Road to Success:

Running a business can be a struggle. My company was in a growth cycle. I had to keep my company growing and guarding against failure, or slipping back in the face of new competition

I developed my business not just for the sake of growth, but to keep it fresh, never losing sight of the core mission. I was always ready to make an adjustment, if my business needed it to improve its position or profits.

I built the company and controlled every aspect of it. My company was run differently than most companies in the corporate world. Most companies are bureaucratic, layered with department heads reporting to a superior and so on and so on. This also adds to having more meetings, some of which are unnecessary and which take time from more important tasks. My company was built to move on opportunity like a lightning rod. Decisions were made quickly and actions were taken at breakneck speed. Most of the companies I competed against were bigger, and that was their disadvantage. Many companies are run by committees or a board of directors, which can slow the decision making process.

My management style was to treat the staff like family, with respect and appreciation being the most important element of my management style. Joel Perry, who became my head of Comedy said of me that I had a talent for picking good people, treating them right and giving them the space to do their best. My management style was different than managers who chose to use more tyrannical method intimation. Some of the greatest managers and super-successful businessmen (famous ones you've have heard of) have used this method, which puts employees on edge and makes them constantly fear for their job. This disgusts me. If you run any size company treat your employees well, respect and appreciation them, they are your biggest asset.

CHAPTER 10

There's No Stopping Us Now

In this Chapter:

- How I created Cutler Comedy Networks.
- The importance of a Unique Selling Proposition.
- How to outthink and outflank your competition.

What next? What programming area could I attack successfully? There were eight comedy services out there, but only two large enterprises and they were all doing a pretty a good job.

Decision making:

Cutler Productions had excellent profits so I decided to put a portion of it to work on developing a new show or service. But what should it be? As successful as I had become in the syndication field, I didn't let it blind me when I took a fresh look at the state of the industry, how the game had changed and how I might make a hefty chunk of change by changing my tactics.

My company was doing well, but the struggle to survive and prosper can be a super challenge. Conditions, events, conflict, surprise and change can happen rapidly.

Principle: Change is inevitable. Resistance is futile. When the static on your radio gets inside your head, it's time to change your mind.

Here's what I discovered, surveying the field:

- Radio syndication had become crowded and fiercely competitive.
- The biggest players (networks and their syndication divisions) owned the biggest stations in the major markets and would sooner place one of their own syndicated shows in the slot than a competitor's, because they'd make more profit. With commercial interests as the prime motivator (not necessarily audience size), the quality of the product wasn't as much of a competitive factor.
- Radio program directors (especially in the bigger markets) had less autonomy to make decisions, especially with the rise of media consolidation and programming consultancies.
- Most "long form" (one to four hours) syndicated shows were relegated to weekend timeslots, and often after midnight, or Sunday mornings, where the potential audience was asleep, at church (or both). With smaller numbers came smaller revenues (advertising rates are based on a cost per thousand listeners).
- Sometimes, in order to get on a station in the top markets, you had to either hire talent that was working at the station and/or pay the station a fee to run the show, much like supermarkets charge food companies a hefty sum just for shelf space.

When the competition is filled with "me too" derivatives of your unique original, your proprietary product has become "commoditized." Once your service or product is seen as a commodity, the only competition is on price and this is when connections or politics trumps the innovation of creation. It's still about filling a need, but price becomes the dominant factor to consumers.

On the other hand, you can step outside the box of convention and outflank the big boys by finding a new niche, and either filling the need for a service or changing the business model, or both.

Most of the comedy services were sold to stations for cash: the stations paid for the service (they saw it as a business expense). At the time, only two were distributed using the barter model. All of them provided produced comedy bits (usually 30 to 60- second features).

A barter comedy service would have valuable commercial spots in morning drive time (5-10 am), which had the largest radio audience, and therefore commanded the highest rates.

The first thing I pondered was how I would differentiate my comedy service from the other services—the unique selling proposition. At the time, all the other services offered only produced comedy bits. I decided to offer the radio morning personalities in America a lot more. In addition to the produced bits we would overnight faxes with topical humor, morning show ideas—like contests, games, news of the day and other features. Cutler also sent out a weekly newsletter that would be filled with still more morning show ideas.

In this way we filled the needs of morning show *producers* and *air-personalities*, not just the program directors. Since we were producers ourselves, we had a built-in understanding of their mindset and their toughest problems on a daily basis. By saving them time and stress and giving them a trustworthy, useful and (to a degree) customizable product with no cash expense, they had a winner. For Cutler to win, we had to absorb a large start-up cost, but because of profits coming in from the other shows, I decided it was worth the risk.

If you're going to laugh, it might as well be all the way to the bank. But seriously, folks: always measure the risk to reward. If the reward ratio is much greater than the risk and the probability for success is high—it's worth taking. A word of caution: make sure you have used the other principles and ideas in this book as well before you make a decision.

Now I went to work on all the comedy elements and features. I made a list of elements like *Sitcom Hell*, a parody of famous sitcoms, song parodies, impersonations of famous politicians and celebrities, and other features that would give the comedy writers guidance. Next, I hired the comedy writers; some went on to bigger things like Alex Herschlag, later to become a writer on *Will and Grace* and one of the show's executive producers; Pat Verrone, who later wrote for the Johnny Carson show; Vic Cohen, who writes for Howie Mandel: and Joel Perry, who later became my head of comedy and an amazing talent. All were work-for-hire. They needed the money so they could stay off the street while they were building their careers. A lot of it was piecework and freelance, but for creative people in Los Angeles, at least it was steady pay and not "spec equity," which pays "nada."

Next was getting the right performers to voice the produced comedy bits. This was new territory for me. I knew what to look for in casting announcers and radio DJ talent better than most, but this was a different cast of "characters." Mark Weingarden, a comedian, helped in finding some of the initial voices and I went around to the comedy clubs to check out others. In the end, I was lucky to find not only talented people but artists who were a pleasure to work with. The voice talents also contributed enormously to the success of *Cutler Comedy Networks*. I paid them fairly and paid them on time (not normally a Hollywood tradition), at the going rate. If it meant they waited on a few less tables and had a chance to ply their craft, it served us both well. (At the end of this book, you'll find the names of the writers, performing artists and staff, who were the reason *Cutler Productions* became successful. Thank you to all of them.)

I was able to get the most of my talent by scheduling them in such a way where we could do multiple bits in a short period of time and paying by the hour rather than by the piece. I thought it was fair and efficient. Nobody complained. Performers' unions have rules to ensure their members aren't unduly exploited. That's only fair, yet sometimes it can work against the self-interests of the performers and the show. If it means there's no show or less of a show because you couldn't hire enough talent, then nobody gets to work and everybody loses. Giant networks, raking in billions, can afford to pay the high rates and still make an obscene profit. Superstars make many times the union rates. The folks getting started, though, need the work. If you're a non-union shop, that doesn't give you permission to take unfair advantage of a competitive and often subjective market for talent. But there's nothing stopping you.

> **Principle: Choose the higher moral ground. You'll stand taller when you honor those whose shoulders you're standing on.**

The people who worked at Cutler were all special to me. We were a family of hard working professionals determined to produce the best shows and services possible. I honor all of them: writers, voice talent, sales people, office personnel and engineers that made *Cutler Productions* and Cutler Comedy Networks successful.

One of them in particular was with me from the beginning to the end of *Cutler Productions*. The engineer who worked for me from 1982 to 1996 was one of the greatest special programming radio engineers ever, Peter Perkins.

> **Principle: You're only as good as the talent you hire. Don't shortchange yourself.**

But we still needed the sales reps (known as station relations people) to clear the programs and services. I worked closely with them and occasionally helped clear a Top 10 market station.

The national advertising sales were handled by Global (a sales company who sold to national advertisers) and Nan Kingsley (who worked for Global), a super salesperson who had great relationships. The comedy networks at the time produced more than half of Global revenues. The company now called Dial Global is a major syndicator and even owns Westwood One Radio Networks.

Now it was time to build the network. Prior to making the decision to do the *Cutler Comedy Network*, my sales people and I made calls to radio stations around the country to find out what they needed and wanted in a comedy service. That information was vital to creating the product.

Research is an important ingredient in your success. You don't need to hire a marketing research firm if you can't afford it. It may be better for you to do it yourself. You'll find out firsthand what your targeted customers want and can then develop benefits and features that serve their needs, enhancing your chances of success.

There's a difference between wants and needs. Don't skew your research so that the two get confused. Many people can't articulate their needs, but can easily verbalize their wants. Read between the lines, listen to the silences. If an obese person says what he wants is another cheeseburger, maybe what he needs is to lose weight.

Cutler Comedy Network was a huge success and the demand for it was staggering. Having launched the first comedy network, I decided now to launch the second comedy network: *Cutler Rock Comedy*, in January, 1990. It too was a success and I decided to package the two networks together to give advertisers bigger ratings and numbers for their advertising, which allowed us to charge higher advertising rates.

Most comedy services were lucky to get five to seven minutes of commercial minutes in morning drive. We asked for 10 minutes—twenty 30-second spots. The demand for our comedy service, even though we were competing with seven other companies, was so strong that it didn't present any problems.

If you can offer your customers more benefits and features than your competitors, you'll finish first.

In the first three years of the comedy networks I ran all the writers' meetings. Pitches (between one and two hundred comedy bits) were presented at our Monday meetings. Although my comedy writers were funnier than me, I chose the final comedy pieces that went to the radio stations. With my on-air background, I had an ear for what I thought stations wanted. Also I had to check every short segment (30-60 Seconds) to make sure the stations wouldn't have any problems with pieces that were too risqué, libelous or too much over the top. All the writers were free-lance and were paid per bit sold. Take a group of 10-15 talented comedy writers, put them in a room, and you have a laugh-fest. I enjoyed working with all of them.

Joel Perry, a gifted comedy writer, and a joy to work with, I chose to be Cutler's head of comedy. He ran the comedy meetings till I sold the company. Fifteen years later, his talent continues to sparkle at Premiere Networks.

1991
MOMENTUM

My business was growing, momentum was building, but in business and war things can change rapidly. It's easy to get caught in the euphoria of success, of dollars pouring in and thinking it has no end. When you start thinking that way, beware, for your future and that of your employees are in danger. You must stay aware of threats and surprises that may appear. In my case: new competition, stations cancelling programs, shows losing their mojo, or talent problems. How do you handle the situation? You take dynamic action. Business is like chess: you plan all your moves ahead of time. True entrepreneurs keep their business from becoming static by constantly developing new projects and services, studying their industry and its current trends, and of course, their competition. Be aware of everything you can control, and have a plan to react to any possible surprises.

Business was now booming, with record revenues and profits. Still I was determined to add more features to our comedy networks.

> **Principle:** If you can "spin off" your brand by adding additional customers with a similar related product, roll it out. If you can package both products as a larger "collective" media buy, you can increase your profits with greater sales and production efficiencies.

I hired Mark Shipper to join the original *Cutler Comedy Network* that catered to mostly Top 40 stations. His daily fax of comedy and gossip added another important service to our growing networks. He was tremendous.

Country, Adult Contemporary and Oldies programmers were calling us to get our Comedy. To accommodate the demand, I added *Cutler Firepower* as the third Comedy network, and tailored that service to Adult Contemporary and Oldies stations. Plus I still had revenues coming in from the two CBS Radio Network shows, *On the Move* and *Cruisin' America*, and Cutler also continued to produce and distribute *Party America*.

There is one business area where you can still hit it big today that wasn't a factor in the early 90's: the Internet. Like the brick and mortar businesses, though, most of these businesses also either fail or fail to deliver a livable income. Though startup fees may be minimal, all the standard principles of good business still apply. As always, the best way to get rich quick is to invent a time machine and then fast forward through all the tough years of getting your business off the ground. Of course, that's not reality. The real key is to meet a need that's not being filled and then fill it. The other way is to take an existing product and do it a lot better than the leader in the field. Example: *Facebook* knocked off *My Space*, which was a hot commodity, till *Facebook* destroyed them.

There are literally millions of web sites out there. But it's the one place where, if you have an original idea, and your site catches on fast, then it's possible to make a profit eventually (but usually not quickly). You must make sure you're capitalized, and you have enough staying power to last for at least three years. The biggest problem when you start a web site: how to attract visitors, and when you do, how do you turn them into revenues. As I told you earlier, make sure your idea is original and provides for a need that isn't being met. The bigger the need you fill, the bigger the potential profit. *Facebook, You Tube* and *Twitter* are web sites that caught fire quickly. The biggest problem with a web site is: how do you make a profit? The last time I checked, despite its phenomenal success, *Facebook* didn't make money for its first five years. It was part of their strategy: build the audience and the dollars would come later. It worked and now it's raining dollars since they learned ways to monetize their zillion visitors. *Twitter* took years to figure out to monetize their site. *You Tube* didn't get their jackpot payday until *Google* bought it.

I started a web site called *RonDiamond.com* for reasons that had nothing to do with business. In the last chapter of this book, I will share that amazing experience with the hopes it helps those of you who are contemplating an internet site.

On the Road to Success:

You can get it if you really want it, but you must give it your all to succeed. Visualize a successful result in your mind. Have a plan of action including strategy (strategic planning) built on tactics. Ask yourself: how will I attract customers, how will I deal with competition? Then anticipate all the obstacles and roadblocks along the way with a variety of means to overcome them. Use your head first, and then jump in with both feet.

It takes time to build momentum, but when it starts, it steam-rolls your way to higher profits. Momentum builds momentum and makes your job easier. I worked for years building my company, working many seventy-hour weeks, and now all that hard work was paying off big time. The start and early years of a business are tough.

This is when it's make it or break it time. Remember more than 50% of all new businesses fail. How can you increase your chances for success? First, make sure you do a feasibility study (Google or Bing this term for more info on how they are done). This will help answer, if there is a need for your product or service. Second, make sure there are enough customers or audience who want your product or service. If it's a location-based business, make sure you have a good one. A good location is a site where your targeted customers frequent often and has excellent parking: example—a mall or a heavy traffic location).

Check out the competition. Ask yourself: what's your USP (unique selling proposition). Hire a good lawyer and accountant, and if you need a consultant, hire one, but make sure he or she has a track record of success. Before you start your business, make sure you have a marketing plan. If you're inexperienced, buy a franchise with a record of success.

Regardless of which road you choose, it's now up to you. Work hard, persevere, and use the ideas and information in this book that you feel comfortable with, and throw in a little bit of luck, and you'll have a higher probability of success.

"Leadership training" they teach in corporations is bogus if it assumes everyone can be a good leader. If that were so, we'd all be leaders and entrepreneurs and there wouldn't be anyone available to hire as employees. You do need, however, to find a healthy level of autonomy to give your employees, so that they have a sense of belonging to the enterprise and the satisfaction of knowing their actions and opinions have a forum for expression and that they, personally, make a difference. Nurture your relationship with your employees: Make them feel like family, treat them well, respect and appreciate them, for they are your greatest asset.

Give your customers what they want and need, and price it within their reach. Make it a goal to have people actually feel delighted to pay for your product. A satisfied customer is a repeat customer. A delighted customer is also a word-of-mouth advertiser for your product.

Networking is an essential part of success in business. Contacts will make your job easier. Non-compete clauses are a double-edged sword. If you think you need your employee to sign one, it may be a good idea, but it also says that you may not trust the relationship going in. Loyalty counts. And if your dream team isn't in the house, you'll need to know how to recruit one from your network of trusted peers.

Business can be a struggle; by its very nature, it's competitive. At its worst, it can be like war. Think of the giant companies that went out of business or went bankrupt.

CHAPTER 11

In this Chapter:

- The staff takes a cruise.
- More joy and sorrow.
- The biggest loss in my life leads me to sell the company.
- For the time being, the end of the journey.

1992
KEYS TO SUCCESS

Business continued to boom as I added a fourth network to the mix: *Cutler Country Comedy*, targeted to the hundreds of Country stations across America. The plan was now to maximize profits. We sold *Cutler Comedy* and *The Rock Comedy Networks* to advertisers targeting 18-34 adults and *Firepower* and *Country* to advertisers targeting 25-54 adults. Each network had two stations in most of the top 172 markets. The four networks had over 1000 morning shows carrying our comedy. The profits continued to climb. Advertisers were happy because our two networks were both delivering huge numbers to them.

There's one thing I haven't shared with you yet. The real key to our success was the amazing morning radio talent in America. Without morning radio personalities, we would never have succeeded. Many of the comedy bits that we produced for them you may have heard, along with millions and millions of people every morning, but if it wasn't for the talents and genius of morning radio personalities across America, *Cutler Comedy* never would have succeeded. Our job was to make good jocks better, and I think we accomplished that.

I always worked to improve our comedy networks. In 1992 we added a talented morning show personality and writer to our fax services (a morning prep newsletter that added more information and entertainment for morning personalities) for stations that were on *Firepower* and the *Country Comedy Networks*: Don Carpenter. He already had radio stations that carried his service. I made a deal with Don for him to join our comedy networks and we offered his daily fax exclusively through Cutler. We more than tripled his station list while adding another important feature to our arsenal of services and features. Don Carpenter and Mark Shipper were a joy to work with. Both were exceptionally talented and contributed significantly to Cutler's success.

Principle: If you can consolidate and collaborate rather than compete, and it's a win for everybody, make a deal. A compromise is a deal, but collaboration is a good deal better.

1993
WHEELING AND DEALING

Our four comedy services continued to do well. It was the last year of *On the Move with Tom Joyner*. ABC went after him in a big way, offering him a great deal of money to do a national daily morning show. It made sense. *On the Move* was a three-hour weekend show, and Tom doing a daily show would provide ABC with 20 hours a week of morning show commercial inventory. They would pay Tom handsomely and he deserved it. There was only one problem: Cutler was making a sizable profit with *On the Move* and I had Tom under contract until 1996. I made a deal with ABC to pay me most of the profits I would have made if we continued the show for those three years and released Tom from his contract. It was a smart move for ABC and Tom, as his new morning show became a phenomenal success. And it was a good deal for me. I was sure glad we had a contract.

Principle: Get a good attorney to write your contracts. Don't create a contract because you distrust the other person. That's no way to start a relationship. Sign a contract because you trust one another and want to document the relationship. In business your personal integrity is like money in the bank.

Scott Shannon, an outstanding radio personality, was doing a countdown show for Westwood One. The show was entertaining but countdown shows were beginning to wane. For years, starting with *American Top Forty with Casey Kasem* and then *The Rick Dees Weekly Top 40*, countdown shows were a stable of weekend programming on Top 40 stations. They were enormous money makers. Westwood One decided to drop Scott's Shannon's countdown show, I had a chance to pick it up and distribute and produce it. I considered Scott one of the greatest talents in radio, but I knew that countdown shows had begun to lose their appeal to many stations. My research showed that listeners were tiring of the well-worn countdown concept. I knew going in the odds were it would fail, but I still thought it was worth a try. I was concerned that Scott would be hard to work with, but actually he was one of the easiest people I ever had the privilege to work with—a gentleman and a mammoth talent. I tried to change the format of a countdown show radically, hoping it would differentiate it from other similar shows. So we changed the countdown from the 40 songs in order, to a countdown where we featured a group countdown; male and female artists competing against each other in separate countdowns that were still based on record sales. Most Top 40 stations at the time carried only one Top 40 countdown show. Dees and Casey's shows were too well-established for us to have a great station line-up.

Scott has an exceptional voice and delivery and did a wonderful job hosting the show, but we had to deal with circumstances beyond our control and the show ended. Today, Scott continues in New York doing his highly-rated morning show. He is a true radio legend.

> **Principle: Sometimes your best efforts will fail, even when you have a good product. If the field you're entering is crowded and demand for your product or service is slowing—don't enter the fray.**

THE JOY AND THE SORROW

January 17, 1994 4:30 AM

I was lying in bed when, all of a sudden the bedroom in my home began to move. There was a sound like a sonic boom and the walls of the room began to dance and the floor shook and I felt I was on an a ride in Disneyland. I'd been in California for 24 years and experienced a few earthquakes, but most were small. They were more fun than scary but this one was different; it felt like the house could collapse. I grabbed my three-year old son, Max, and Lori, and we ran into the street. Virtually every neighbor was outside. We were all shell-shocked. Hundreds of houses and businesses had major damage, but not in our neighborhood. We were lucky; we had only minor damage. The earthquake was centered in Northridge, six miles north of our offices. Our office building had extensive damage.

At 6 am, I decided to go and check the damage. I drove the seven miles to our office building. The damage was severe and the power was out. The elevators didn't work so to get to my third floor office I had to crawl on my hands and knees to go up the damaged stairs. I was worried, first for the safety of my staff, and second for the 2000 radio stations depending on us to get their shows. I tried to get into my office, but a cabinet had fallen, blocking the entrance. The building was a hazard and we were told we shouldn't go in. But the show had to go on. We have never failed to deliver a show on time to our stations, but this time it seemed impossible. I told you I had a great staff. One by one they too crawled up the stairs. By 8:30 the entire staff showed up. They helped open the door to my office. I had an Apple computer that was destroyed, but my main computer was fine. Peter and the other engineers checked the studios, which had only had minor damage, quickly repaired. Everyone chipped in to make sure our offices were operational again.

I loved my staff and that day they showed me why. Miraculously we delivered our shows on time. What loyalty. What a special talented and dedicated group of professionals. We had minor damage, but no one got hurt and the shows went on as scheduled.

In December that year, for our Christmas party, I took the entire staff on a three night, four-day Mexican cruise. Loyalty is a two-way street.

I hadn't seen the Cutler staff since 1997. In 2008, most of the staff surprised me by showing up for the book signing of my first novel *The Secret Scroll* at a neighborhood Barnes & Noble in Calabasas.

1994 was another good year, with revenues and profits increasing from the four comedy networks. Cruisin' America finished its long run and Tom Joyner had left for ABC Radio Networks. For the first time in twelve years we didn't have a show on one of the major networks, but that didn't stop us from having a banner year.

> **Principle: Business is like chess, you have to plan your moves way ahead. I had prepared since 1990 for the day Cutler would be totally independent. Although all the shows we licensed to the networks were profitable, we made more profits going it alone.**

I decided to continue *On the Move* with Urban air personality Russ Parr who, at the time was tearing up the Dallas market. Russ did a wonderful job. The show enjoyed some success and was profitable.

Walt Love at the time was the Urban Radio editor at *Radio & Records*, the leading radio trade publication, and a well-known and respected radio personality. Walt's show had ended a successful run at Westwood One. He was looking for another company to syndicate his show, so he joined *Cutler Productions* with the Walt Love Show. Walt was surprisingly easy to work with and brought along his producer, Dianna Rose, from Westwood. The Walt Love Show was syndicated and produced by *Cutler Productions* and ran until the company was sold.

1994 was the sixth straight record-breaking year of revenues and profits. It was an exceptionally good year for business, and time for our Christmas party and a chance again to show my appreciation to the people who helped make it happen, my staff. We all took a three-day cruise to Mexico. What a great party. What a great year in business. But life is full of both joy and sorrow.

Sorrow showed its painful and ugly face. I lost my father, Martin Cutler, on March 13th. On October 14th, my mother, Sadie had a horrific auto accident that caused her misery and suffering for the rest of her life.

> **Principle: Your parents do the best job they're capable of doing. Take the good things they taught you and learn from the mistakes they made and your life will be fuller.**

My Aunt Betty had lived with my mother for 18 years before my mother's accident. After her accident my mom wasn't able to take care of her. Aunt Betty had senile dementia and was put in a state institution, not a great place for her. When I found out, I took a plane to Philadelphia, and had her released and took her back to California. I took her to a private nursing home near my house so I could watch over her. Aunt Betty was the most generous and loving person of her generation and, if you remember, she's the one who gave me the $25 to start it all.

> **Principle: Make sure you take care of the people who took care of you, especially if they're your blood, in their time of need. You'll find it the most rewarding experience.**

With the death of my dad, the serious injury to my mom, and my Aunt Betty's Alzheimers, I didn't think things could get worse. Was I ever wrong.

1995
THE SADDEST YEAR OF MY LIFE

Cutler Productions experienced the seventh straight record-breaking year of revenues and profits. The year was going great. Business was above my expectations. When you're on a tranquil sea and everything seems right with your world, life can still change suddenly. The year was moving along and we were making plans for our annual Christmas party.

Monday, November 20, 1995

The worst day of my life, the day that changed everything.

I worked the entire day and had a business dinner that evening. I arrived home and sat on the couch. I had the unexplainable feeling that something was wrong. At 7:50, the phone rang; it was my ex-wife Judy telling me that my 22-year old son, Seth had died in a tragic accident. I first felt disbelief; I had seen Seth the day before. Then it hit me, pain radiated through my chest, and I thought I would pass out. I was in shock—I never felt pain like this before. Seth was gone. This was one problem I couldn't solve. I had lost a parent, but nothing prepared me for the loss of a child. I was numb. Thanksgiving came three days later, and to this day, I never look forward to it.

Principle: Business may be a way to make money and prosper, but the real riches are in those we love.

I decided to devote more time to my four-year-old son, Max, and the rest of my family.

I was devastated and decided the time to sell *Cutler Productions* was now. I knew this decision would cost millions of dollars in the future, but the future without the ones you love is meaningless. I sold the company for half of what I felt it was worth.

Premiere Radio Networks, a public company, and my main

124

comedy competition, was interested in buying Cutler (and getting rid of me as their competition). I was exhausted, depressed and ready for a change. Negotiations started with Premiere. In the meantime another company came in and offered me double what Premiere was offering me, but they asked me to wait two more months before they could buy Cutler. They needed the time for final approval from their multi-billion dollar parent company.

> **Principle: When it's time to get out and you can live with your exit strategy—get out.**

I was more than ready. I took Premiere's offer of 8.5 million in cash, plus receivables, which added another million dollars. I definitely could have gotten more, but I wasn't greedy, and after 36 years of working my tail off it was time to take a break. My concern was making sure my staff didn't lose their jobs. Premiere agreed to keep all my employees and also agreed to their raises for 1997. All my employees had their profit shares accelerated. Premiere kept their promises to my employees.

I had taken $15,000 to more than $10,000,000—a lot more, if you count the profits Cutler made over the years.

And you can do it too. I'm an average guy who worked hard, found needs and filled them, and hired the right people who were talented and delightful to work with. I encourage you to follow your dreams. You must have a burning desire to succeed, be honest and always give one hundred percent. Life's too short, so make the best of it.

On the Road to Success:

Always keep working to improve your product or services. Never stand still; if you do your company will stop moving forward.

Give your customers great service and make sure you meet their needs. Good customer service is essential for success in business. Treat everyone well—it's the most important thing you can do in business and life.

Appreciate the people you do business with: customers, vendors, employees, independent contractors and most of all your family. If you are serious about it and mean it, pay them sincere compliments, which will brighten their day. Always be appreciative of people who enhance your life. There's too little appreciation given in business and in this world. And if you try to fake it, they'll see right through you.

Principle: No one can do it alone.

CHAPTER 12

Ron Diamond.com

Let the Good Times Roll

In this Chapter:

- The return of Ron Diamond.
- Building an internet site on the cheap, at least initially.
- How to create a monster site.

25 years had passed since I had done a Ron Diamond radio show. In truth, I never appreciated the character. Although I loved the music and the jam-packed dances filled with kids having a great time, I didn't like being a big fish in a small pond. Although I saw myself as a minor celebrity (surprisingly), I didn't like being in the spotlight. I didn't really appreciate the effect I was having on others. I had no idea what my listeners thought of me and, more importantly, if I had made a difference in their lives. For the next 25 years, when I thought about the Diamond character or did some of the old sayings, it seemed trivial and unimportant, almost a joke.

It all changed when, two months after Seth's death, to my surprise, WOGL, the Oldies station in Philadelphia asked me to be part of their Oldies Greats reunion. I was shocked. They invited all the big-name air-personalities who had been on two legendary Top 40 stations, WIBG and WFIL, as well as their current WOGL air staff (some had worked at the aforementioned stations). I was the maverick. I was the first Rock in Roll air-personality on FM radio in Philly, a year before the national explosion of FM rock stations across the country. They invited 30 big-named Philly air-personalities including Hy Lit, Dr. Don Rose, George Michael and Joey Reynolds, to name a few. I worked on WIFI and WTTM in Trenton. WTTM served three of the seven counties which made-up the Philadelphia metro market.

In 1971, John Gehron was named program director of WCAU-FM (later WOGL), and his first decision was to choose a format for the station. He studied the Arbitron book of spring 1970 and found in the seven to midnight ratings WTTM (and the Ron Diamond show) was the number two-rated station in teens and women 18-24. This was despite the station covering less than 50% of the market. By then I had left for California. John saw a major need and hole in the market, and decided to make WCAU-FM an Oldies station.

Back to the Oldies reunion—Scott, the program director, knew of me because he carried *Cutler Productions'* shows. He didn't know I had been a Philly air-personality. But Harvey Holiday and Bob Pantano, two of their disc jockeys told him about me. Scott was apprehensive about inviting me to the reunion. But he decided to do so with the provision that I do part of Harvey's Sunday night show and do the 7-9 pm portion which would close the reunion (7-9PM on Sunday night is the lowest-rated time period of the week). I wasn't sure I wanted to go to the reunion. I hadn't done the Ron Diamond show in years. I then thought about my son Seth who had died two months before the invitation. He had always wanted me to bring back the Diamond character. I was in mourning and I figured this might be one way to deal with my grief. Seth had given me a gift and I took it, deciding to bring back Ron Diamond one more time.

May 10, 1996 (Mother's Day)

Most of the 30 air-personalities improvised and did what they normally did. Not me, I had produced some of radio's most successful national shows, so now it was time to give Philly a show they would never forget. Fired up by the spirit of Seth and determined to not let him down, I prepared for the show. I decided I would return the audience back to 1969; not only present the music and the Ron Diamond exclusives (songs that nobody else played) but also recreate the sights, places and moments of that time. I made up jingles, created comedy bits and I was ready for blast-off, but was still concerned I might bomb. What I didn't know at the time was that Scott the Program Director had told Harvey that he would call at 7:30, and if I sucked, Harvey was to yank me and take over the show. Scott had no idea what I had in mind.

My family had flown in with me from California. My sisters, aunts, cousins and friends in Philly listened. I arrived at WOGL studios on the Main Line armed with carts full of jingles, comedy bits, drops and background music. I opened the show telling the audience that my real name was Ron Cutler and I was doing the show dedicated to my son Seth, who had died six months earlier. He wanted me to do this (it was emotional) and after 25 years, I was doing this. I said, "Some of you know me and many of you may not, but in the next two hours you will." And with that, the jingle "The Diamond's back and he's going to play the music," the show started. The phones went crazy. Scott called at 7:30 and said, "Keep him on."

The response was overwhelming. I ended the show in tears. I told the audience I hoped I did Seth proud. I thought I had given it my best shot and delivered the goods for Seth. He gave me one last great gift, which became a harbinger of what yet was to come.

129

I told you before I didn't think Ron Diamond made a difference. I never told the audience where I was broadcasting from. I left the studio and went through the lobby. To my surprise, it was jammed with people wanting to shake my hand and tell me how I inspired them and how they loved my show back then, and how I made a difference in their lives. I was shocked. The Ron Diamond character, who I had avoided, except to joke about him, was far more important to my audience than I ever knew. The next day, emails and phone calls poured in to WOGL about my show.

When I left Philadelphia for California in October 1970, I began a new career. Tired of being an air personality I crept into the shadows of backstage, where I felt comfortable. I became a producer. From then on I would be in the background. Most people who listened to the shows I produced and created never knew who I was—and I liked that.

As I told you earlier, my late son Seth always wanted me to do Ron Diamond again. (I didn't want to do it because I thought Diamond's time had passed.) Seth was in his late teens when he started asking. He heard tapes of the old Ron Diamond shows and loved them.

Now it was 1999 and I was still grieving for Seth. I decided to handle my grief by creating an internet site in Seth's memory. I called my old friend Don Goldberg, who was working for Microsoft's internet streaming media group at the time. He was able to see the online landscape through a radio and syndication background and a technological media high ground better than just about anyone I knew.

I would pick the music, select the themes, drops, jingles and bits, block the show, engineer and be the personality. I would also upload the shows to our server in Colorado. I was in Los Angeles, Don in Seattle and our server in Colorado. Oh, the miracle that's the Internet. Don was in charge of editorial pages, writing text on the pages and everything else.

Ron Diamond.com debuted in November 1999. That month 900 unique visitors listened to my shows. Unique listeners are the number of listeners that actually visit the site. They're only counted once, even if they visit the site many times. I started out doing one show a week, but as the demand grew by February, I did a new show every day. I was doing the site out of love and for altruistic reasons. Later, I would realize that, even when you do something for reasons other than business, it's still business, and surprises can happen. I would realize my motivation for doing the site was one of the reasons for its success. The numbers would exceed my expectations, which was easy to do because my expectations were so low. I didn't realize at the time that Seth was giving me an enormous gift.

I had no promotion budget. One of the gifts of the web is that, if your site is unique and it's well done, sooner or later people will likely find you. You'd think that buzz is easy to start on the Internet if you have a product that is unique, different and exciting. Not necessarily, though, and even if you do, what do you do for an encore? Even then, the Internet had thousands of audio sites, from the broadcast of local radio shows to sites that were primarily database-driven jukeboxes.

Ron Diamond.com was one of the first personality sites presenting music on the Internet. The music spanned from 1957-1989. At the time, Oldies radio stations were playing music from 1957-1972. There were many sites playing Oldies music, but they were all either nondescript jukeboxes or amateur web casts.

I blocked the show, selected the music and show themes, produced and voiced every show.

RonDiamond.com featured a lively personality who communicated with the listeners, mixing comedy with the best music of all time. Each song was programmed for emotional impact. My job was to set up each song so to enhance the listeners' pleasure. Each song was programmed to flow into the next.

All the shows had themes. Listeners could look at a list of songs featured on each program and select the one that matched their music tastes. If you liked Oldies, Disco, Classic Rock, Soul and R&B, Doo Wop, or Hits from the Eighties, you could find them all. At the time, RonDiamond.com had a unique selling proposition. Also, because we played Oldies, the archived shows, rather than become outdated, actually added to the selection of appropriate material.

Each month the audience grew exponentially. Suddenly, I was deluged with hundreds, then thousands of emails. I was working 90 hours a week and beginning to burn myself out. But every time I received an email from an ill person telling me what the show meant to them, it revitalized my energy.

One of the great advantages of the Internet is that it's one of the greatest ways to build buzz.

Through Don's resources at Microsoft, we were able to meet with the people at Windowsmedia.com. They had a technology to "evangelize" (that's what they call it, folks) and were looking to team up with unique and well-produced audio content providers. What's more, we negotiated that if they gave us good placement on their site, we'd give them an exclusive, in that our streams would be delivered in their format (and not the competitor's Real Media). At that time Microsoft and Real Media were the two major services competing for audio delivery on the web. Microsoft needed audio content and we were there to fill the need.

> **Principle: Everybody needs somebody sometime, but the gates of opportunity (even if they're Bill's Gates) don't open by themselves. If you've got a good idea, don't be so intimidated you won't ask for a meeting with the big guys, and when you do, meet with the decision makers.**

The buzz on RonDiamond.com started when MSN (Microsoft Network) started mentioning my special music theme for the day. At least once a week, MSN.com promoted one of my shows. The buzz ignited other sites that began mentioning the show and how special the site was. All of a sudden bandwidth came into play.

You see, as Don puts it, streaming media (at the time, anyway) wasn't "broadcasting" but "longcasting" in that you cast your net over the internet one stream at a time. The more listeners, the more bandwidth was used. In traditional broadcasting, one cast reaches everyone over the air at once. So, the initial costs in broadcasting are huge: purchasing a station's license, building a studio, installing a transmitter and all the other attendant costs. Once you start broadcasting, however, your transmission expenses are the same whether you reach one person or a million. On the internet, however, the inverse is true. It costs little to get in the game, but the more listeners tune in, the more it costs.

Principle: Beware of the hidden side of technology. You could become a victim of your own success.

My bandwidth costs skyrocketed. I paid thirty cents per megabit for bandwidth, a decent rate at the time, but expensive by today's standards. (The cost of bandwidth has dropped substantially since 2000). Throughout that year visitors to the site drastically increased each month. In the year 2000, 3,000,000 unique visitors clicked on to RonDiamond.com. In the month of December 2000 alone, there were more than 80,000,000 hits.

No one expected such success, especially our bandwidth provider who was shocked by the enormous amount of bandwidth we used.

Don had the common sense to know there were ways to conserve bandwidth. At the time, many competing internet "stations" were playing music in stereo and at much greater encoding rates, thereby jacking up their costs as much as fourfold (at a time most people were still using slow modems, anyway). We encoded at a lower (but acceptable) bit rate and in mono. After all, we were playing Oldies, and we knew people clicked our way for the content, not the fidelity. Microsoft probably preferred that we used the best fidelity to show off their technology, but they weren't paying the bill.

> **Principle: While you should never shortchange yourself, don't feel compelled to pay for more than you need.**

I was paying for three terabytes (3 trillion megabits of bandwidth)—a staggering number. The cost was thousands each month. And the site was primarily an audio site. Pictures, video and audio add significantly to bandwidth costs. Answering emails became a full-time job, but even on the internet, in the digital space, personal contact is the key to customer retention.

Use a database to keep track of your customers, but use a real person (and a good one) to help with problems and questions. It might be more efficient to be treated like a number, but it's no way to treat a customer.

The site had gotten so big so quickly that I was burning out. Remember, this site was not initially designed to be a business, but a labor of love. I was paying all the expenses, which also had gone into the stratosphere. I thought about monetizing the site, but never had a chance to do it. In mid-December I received a letter from the RIAA, (the Recording Industry Association of America) claiming that I was not in compliance with the Digital Millennium Copyright Act of 1998 (DMCA).

When I started RonDiamond.com there were no real guidelines. From the day I launched the site, I paid ASCAP, BMI and

SESAC, the music publishers. RIAA was going after NAPSTER, a site where you could download music for free. I streamed my music at 20K, making it hard, if not impossible, to download. I respect intellectual property. And many record stores around the country wrote that I was positively influencing sales.

The DMCA was designed to stop piracy, which I applaud, but instead, it was the act that led to falling record sales, and the record industry blew an opportunity to use the Internet to its advantage. The record companies lobbied the Clinton administration and Congress for its passage and by doing that, ultimately shot themselves in the collective foot. I was told I couldn't front-announce songs (announcing the title and artist before playing the song), which seems to me to be a violation of free speech. I would be restricted from playing more than two songs an hour from a particular artist. I couldn't publish the list of songs for each show on the site, which was a guide for listeners to choose programs that matched their tastes. I would agree with this if listeners were downloading music, but they weren't. We were streaming at 20K, not 44K. Out of the thousands of emails I received, there never was one that mentioned they had copied our songs. Besides if you liked the song, you would want to buy it to get the best quality.

The RIAA was nice to me in that they gave me 90 days to make a deal with the record companies. I would have to go to each one of them for permission. I had spent tens of thousands of dollars, was exhausted, and in January, I closed the site. The site was so popular that the Program Director of Sirius at the time asked if I was interested in having a channel. They were just starting out and projected only 30,000 subscribers their first year. I had many more listeners, I was tired and decided not to take the offer.

I regret now that I never shared the above with the listeners of RonDiamond.com. I simply disappeared.

Here's what you can learn from my experience:

What to do before you start:

If you have a unique idea that isn't being done on the Internet and there is a market for it—go for it.

Make sure you have a solid business plan based on reality and not some industry projection hyped by the promise of technology.

Clearly define your target audience and how you're going to reach them.

Marketing:

Use social networks like *Facebook, Twitter* and *LinkedIn* to spread the word.

Make sure you have an email campaign to sites (and their site producers) that can help you spread the word. If you can make personal contact with the producer, you have a better chance at visibility.

You can use email blasts, but if you do, make them funny and entertaining (and short, without large attachments—instead, drive the traffic to your site with a pithy tease).

Use forums and newsgroups to promote your site.

Promote on sites that target the same customers that you are targeting.

Business Operations:

Choose a great name for your site—make it catchy (Of course you'll build your brand on the content and utility value of the site and not solely on the name).

Do a list of your costs and expenses and a preliminary financial statement. Also include in this an educated guess of what revenues you forecast for your first three years (all part of pro-forma statement).

Decide on the number of employees you'll need. Make a list of their responsibilities and compensation.

Decide where revenues will come from (very important).
Advertising—
Your site's advertising is sold through: Google Ad sales, a sales rep firm, or you try to sell it yourself (difficult).
Merchandising—
This is when you sell merchandise. It could be books, tee shirts, clothes, records, or anything that can be tied in to your site, or you send your visitors to another site to buy a particular product and you receive a commission.
Subscriptions—
This is when you charge a monthly or annual fee to visitors of your site, or a special premium for access to parts of your site (Example: certain stock services, usually subscription, and ESPN, with sections you pay a premium for to get the information).
Premium services—
Similar to subscriptions.
Co-op advertising—
This is where one of the vendors you do business with will pay part of the advertising cost.
Memberships—
This is when you charge a membership fee to access your site. Usually charged on a monthly or annual basis.
Affiliates—
This is where you receive a small commission (usually 2-10%) for sending your site's visitors to another site.
Even sites with millions of visitors are struggling for revenues. Brainstorm unique ways to build revenue.
The above is just a starting point. You can investigate further by using the Internet, books, trade groups and organizations and

experts. But beware of "experts." As we used to say in radio, "a consultant is a person who, when you ask him what time it is, will look at your watch and tell you."

Watch your watch, because timing is everything.

A FEW FINAL THOUGHTS
AND THANKS

We're all in some sort of business, whether you are a student struggling to get good grades, a person who works for an existing business of any type, someone dreaming of starting up his own business, or a current business owner. And any way you look at it, we're all in this crazy business called life.

I loved writing this book. My main goal was to jar your brain into new actions or make you think of new ways to handle your problems. Hopefully it will help to make a difference in some small way and improve your life.

Throughout life, I have strived to be the best I can be. I push myself to my limits. If I can succeed, so can you. I hope someday I can do a seminar (low cost or no cost) that will fire you up to go for it. I wish I had had someone who could have been my mentor. I didn't have any formal training, but I still succeeded. I've created the web site *RonCutlerbooks.com* to be a helpful resource, giving you additional information and assisting you with problems you may encounter.

I'd like to give special thanks to these exceptionally talented people: John Paine (my editor), Jeff Gelb (who looked over every page of this book and gave me valuable guidance), and my friend for over 50 years, Don Goldberg, for his generous contributions to the first draft of the book.

My career started with record hops (teenage dances). From 1962-1970, more than one million teenagers danced at my dances. Many times I think about those dancers and see their smiling faces on the dance floor. I cherish these memories and thank them for being a part of my life and the joy they brought me.

I would also like to thank the tens of thousands of listeners who were the first to jump to FM in Philly when only 15% had

FM radio, and you chose to switch from AM to FM and listen to me on WIFI. You helped launch the FM rock craze. I loved sharing the music I played and presenting the wildest show on radio (I was young and uninhibited) at the time (think Stern without the scatological humor). My show mixed the best Top 40 music with Oldies, plus the music no one else played: back then that was the Ron Diamond Show. At that time, the Oldies format didn't yet exist on radio across America.

Thank you to all the listeners of KOME in San Jose, which also served the San Francisco market and made it into a legendary station. I was learning at the time to run a business, but thanks to the staff of KOME for helping with the lessons I learned that I have used the rest of my life. With all the ups and down and catastrophes, we still survived and built a great station (and it would've made a great sitcom).

Thanks to all of you that went to the *Fox Theatre* in San Jose and to those who partied at *Bahama Mama's* in Culver City and *Dillon's* in the Westwood part of Los Angeles.

As I write this, I miss the talented wonderful people who made my days at Cutler so special. I miss them so much. Allow me to start off with the people I had the pleasure of working with every day:

My office manager and right arm, Shelly Brubaker; the head of comedy, Joel Perry; my station relations team of Mike Stafford, David Brandalino, and Charlie Quinn. The engineering team of: Peter Perkins, Dick Schroder, Warren Harkins, Glen Gordon, and Ron Shapiro.

A thank you to the talented air-personalities who hosted the shows (in alphabetical order): Cousin Brucie, Rick Dees, Rachel Donahue, Tom Joyner, Walt Love, Dave McQueen, Russ Parr, Jimmy Roberts, Scott Shannon, Dick Summers, Chuck Southcott, Jay Thomas and Madeline Vlasic.

The following show producers helped *Cutler Productions* on

the road to success: Howard R. Cohen, Peter Hartz, Ken Cauthern, and Janis Hahn.

A thank you to the following special people who in one way or another contributed to my success: Dick Clark, Howie Gillman, Mel Gollub, Mel Karmazin, Nan Kingsley, Bob Kipperman, Randy Lane, Peter Lescas, Susan Love, Frank Murphy, Norm Pattiz, and Tom Rounds and also ABC, CBS and Westwood One Radio Networks.

Below are the names of the writers and performers that helped make Cutler Comedy Networks so successful. They made a great contribution to our success. I'm grateful and thankful to all performers and writers that made Cutler Comedy super successful and if you are missing from this list, my apologies. Below are the names of some of the most talented performers and writers in Los Angeles:

Mary Kay Bergman (performer)
Don Carpenter (writer)
Donna Cherry (performer)
Gil Christner (producer, writer, performer)
Jenifer Cihi (performer)
Jenny Church (writer)
Vic Cohen (writer)
Marianne Curan (performer)
Stephen DeLello (writer, producer)
Chuck Duran (music)
Greg Eagles (performer)
Bill Farmer (performer)
Rosie Reeves (writer, performer, co-producer)
Robert Morgan Fisher (writer, performer)
Ralph Garman (performer)
Joey Gaynor (performer)
Howie Gold (performer)

James Grant Goldin (writer)
Jess Harnell (performer)
Alex Herschlag (writer)
Jack Kenny (performer)
Janis Liebhart (performer)
Wendy MacKenzie (performer)
Kerrigan Mahan (performer)
John Mammoser (writer)
Lori Mark (performer)
Mark McCracken (writer)
Charles Meyer (writer)
James Napoli (writer)
Deena Norian (performer)
Brendan O'Brien (performer)
Val Paterson (aka Papas) (performer)
Sue Peahl (performer)
Mel Powell (writer)
Albert Perrotta (writer)
Joel Perry (writer, producer)
John Roarke (performer)
Maria Elena Rodriguez (writer)
Allen Ross (performer)
Larita Shelby (performer)
Mark Shipper (writer)
Steve Stoliar (writer, performer)
Doug Stone (writer)
Rob Trow (performer)
Mike Tullberg (writer, sometime performer)
Karri Turner (performer)
Ralph Votrian (performer)
Jim Ward (performer)
Wally Wingert (performer)
Jim Wise (performer)
The majority of my career was spent in radio. I love radio

and particularly have tremendous affection for all radio disc jockeys and personalities. A special thank you to them and the more than 3000 radio stations that carried *Cutler Productions* products, and their general managers.

I also enjoyed working with the program directors, morning air-personalities and producers. Again, my sincere thank you for your help in the success of Cutler programs and services. It couldn't have happened without you.

Thank you to the 3,000,000 unique visitors that listened to RonDiamond.com at a time when it was hard to listen to Internet audio and also thanks for the thousands of emails you sent me. I apologize for never saying goodbye to you. And I thank my late son, Seth, who inspired me to revisit Ron Diamond.

A man is only as good as the woman behind him. For the last 31 years that woman has been my wife, Lori. She gave me the space to be me and supported me through all these adventures. She is a special person, and I'm glad I was lucky enough to find her.

I wrote the first draft of this book in spring of 2009 as a high school graduation gift for my son Max. Max had already made the decision, back in kindergarten that he wanted to be an entrepreneur. I also thought it would be nice to write it for my older son, Jason, who's in investments, but also an aspiring entrepreneur.

I gave additional copies of the book to four of the sales people at my local Barnes and Noble. They liked it and thought I should have it published (this was an unedited version of the first draft). I felt the time wasn't right; having spent the previous year in the publishing world I was tired, so I decided against it.

I kept reading about the country's economic crisis and all the people who were suffering. In late 2011, I started to write the second draft, then the third and finally the final draft (the one you are reading). My motivation this time was different; I wrote it because I wanted to help people, inspire them, and present ideas and principles that would impact their lives. I hope it does.

Thank you all for sharing my life. I put my heart and soul into this book. I hope I delivered an experience that not only entertained you, but will enhance your life and your business. Thanks again for taking the time to read my book.

May your life be happy and successful!

If you need more info, help or ideas, go to
www.Roncutlerbooks.com.

Made in the USA
Charleston, SC
20 September 2012